Contents:

Dedication:

This book is dedicated to the cooks in my life.

My Grandma Chaya Kilstein was my cooking inspiration. She could take a small portion of a recipe and identify the ingredients in their exact proportions. She cooked completely by feel and never used a measuring cup in her life.

My mother Harriet Kilstein loved to follow intricate recipes. Baking was her specialty and she mailed her cakes to her grandchildren all around the world. Her honey cake was world class. (She said the Holiday Honey Cake included in this book was almost as good as her own.)

My wife Chana Abehsera Kilstein created many of the recipes in this book. She brings new tastes to the kitchen. Her recipes combine flavors from many cultures into an incredible sensory experience.

With Thanks to:

Kim Howerton for joining me in the vision of CompletelyKeto.

The Unsung Moderators of Completely Keto who give of themselves every single day.

Brooke Arnold for her work in the layout of this book.

Brandy Arnold for her assistance in publication of this book.

Sandra Parache, my assistant of many years, for making sure everyone who pre-ordered this book received it.

And finally, to all the members of CompletelyKeto who have spread the word about our fantastic site, recipes, and Facebook groups.

Introduction:

"You have Syndrome X," the doctor told me. "That's why you can't seem to lose weight no matter what diet you follow."

I had no clue what Syndrome X was. My doctor smiled. "You of all people should know how to look it up on the computer. It's also called Metabolic Syndrome."

That night I read article after article on a series of medical websites. A huge number of American's had metabolic syndrome and I had never heard of it. By the end of the evening, I knew I had a problem I had never heard of. I was insulin resistant.

Fate led me to the offices of a specialist who subjected me to a battery of blood tests. Frankly I'm amazed anything was left after they finished!

I discovered that not only was I pre-diabetic but all of my hormones were completely out of balance. My doctor told me that my enemy was sugar in all forms. I left his office on a new low carb diet.

Over time my hormones started to balance but due to the insulin sensitivity the scale moved – in the wrong direction. That's when I decided to take action and started Keto. In a year I had shed nearly 40 pounds, gained muscle and was stronger than ever in my life.

Once I started Keto I teamed up with an old friend Kim Howerton and started CompletelyKeto.com and a series of Facebook groups that total nearly 300,000 members.

Our groups have become incredibly active. We have approximately 500,000 posts a month. We have helped tens of thousands of people reach their goals. We hope we can help you.

You may contact me via completelyketo.com.

- Dr. Harlan Kilstein

Nutrition Information:

It was minutes after my first recipe was published that people started talking about how they changed it. They changed the ingredients, the cooking time, how long the ingredients defrosted, number of servings, and more.

It was like playing the game of telephone when you whisper a message in your friend's ear. By the time you get to the last person in the line, the message is entirely changed.

That's what happens with the recipes I publish.

I do not include nutritional information with my recipes because I know how widely they are changed.

To track your macros, use an app like MyFitnessPal and add your own recipes. Do not count sugar alcohols such as xylitol, swerve, or Lakanto. These are not digested by the body.

Once you calculate the macros to the recipes – the way YOU prepare them, they are yours forever.

Tracking your macros is one of the secrets to success in Keto.

Get my FREE daily Keto recipes at completelyketo.com

A Discount for You!

You will see throughout this cookbook that we refer to FoxHill products. They are made by our friend Julie at FoxHillKitchens.com

If you miss bagels, rolls, sliders, or croutons, FoxHill is about to become YOUR best friend, too.

Use the coupon code harlan (lower case only) for
15% off everything, and free shipping when six packages of any combination are ordered.

My freezer is always filled with FoxHillKitchens.com bagels.

CompletelyKeto Cookbook

Recipes You'll Swear Aren't Keto

CompletelyKeto Cookbook
Recipes You'll Swear Aren't Keto
by Harlan Kilstein

ISBN-13: 978-0-692-07820-4 (OTC Publishing Corp)

Disclaimer:
You should always work with a doctor knowledgeable about Keto. Your doctor can determine if the Keto diet is safe for you. We always recommend you listen to your physician.

CompletelyKeto

Salads & Starters

Israeli Salad

1. Dice onion, tomatoes, and cucumbers
2. Add olive oil
3. Salt
4. Pepper
5. Stir together
6. Top with parsley

Ingredients:

1 Large onion
1 Tsp Pink Himalayan salt
1/2 Tsp Pepper
1 Large tomato
2 Large cucumbers
3 Tbs olive oil
Sprig of parsley to garnish

Servings: 4-6

Quick and Easy Chef Salad

1. Cut up all veggies and lay out on a platter
2. Place slices of turkey and corn beef on top and place egg and olives around
3. Mix all dressing ingredients together, store in a small mason jar, and serve salad chilled with dressing on the side

Ingredients:

1/2 Pound thin-sliced corn beef
1/2 Pound thin-sliced turkey
1/2 Red pepper sliced thin
1/2 Green pepper sliced thin
1 Tomato Sliced in wedges
2 Eggs boiled and peeled and sliced in wedges
8 Black olives pitted
6 Oz romaine lettuce cut into small pieces
6 Radishes cut up

Dressing:
1 Cup Primal Kitchen Mayo
1/2 Cup Swerve
1/4 Cup apple cider vinegar
1/4 Cup Homemade
    Ketchup (pg. 156)
1/4 Cup light olive oil
1 Tsp black pepper
1 Garlic clove, minced
1 Tsp pink Himalayan salt
3/4 Tsp dry mustard
3/4 Tsp paprika
Cayenne pepper to taste

Servings: 4

Spinach & Strawberry Salad

1. Wash spinach thoroughly and dry in a salad spinner
2. Place in a bowl
3. Cut strawberries into very small pieces and spread over spinach
4. Toast walnuts and chop very small and drop over spinach and strawberries
5. Cut feta into small cubes or crumble feta cheese all over your salad
6. Combine all ingredients for dressing and mix well in a jar and pour over each individual salad as you plate

Ingredients:

Salad:
15 Oz Fresh Spinach
5 Oz Feta cheese
6 Oz Fresh Strawberries
4 Oz Toasted Walnuts, chopped

Dressing:
Juice of 1 lemon
2 Tbs Extra virgin olive oil
1/2 Tsp Pink Himalayan Salt
1 Tbs Swerve Granular
Pinch of black pepper

Serves: 4

Sour Cream Cucumber And Dill Salad

1. Slice each cucumber in halves lengthwise
2. Cut each cucumber into half circle slices about 1/4 inch thick
3. Place in a bowl
4. Add sour cream, salt, dill, lemon juice, garlic and onion slices
5. Toss to combine flavors well
6. Serve chilled

Ingredients:

3 English cucumbers
2 Cloves fresh garlic, minced
3 Tbs fresh dill chopped
Juice of half a lemon
1/2 Red onion sliced very thin
1 1/2 Cups sour cream
1 1/2 Tsp Sea salt

Serves: 6

Blackened Chicken Salad

1. Using a tenderizer, hammer each piece of chicken between two sheets of parchment paper
2. Dip each piece of chicken into poultry seasoning on both sides, evenly
3. Heat up skillet on medium-high heat and add olive oil
   Place hammered chicken in skillet and sear on each side for 3-5 minutes
4. Remove and set aside
5. Mix salad dressing in a jar or small bowl
6. Plate salad and then place tenderized & blackened chicken on top and pour dressing over

Ingredients:

Chicken:
4 Pieces 0f 6 oz chicken
3 Tbs Olive oil
Poultry Seasoning

Salad:
1 whole head of lettuce
        or a bag of spring greens
2 Ripe avocados, cut in half
        and sliced thin
1 English cucumber, sliced thin
1 Whole red onion, chopped into small cubes
1 Basket of cherry tomatoes, sliced in halves

Dressing:
4 Tbs Olive oil
Juice of one fresh lemon
1 Tsp Pink Himalayan Salt
Pinch of ground black pepper

Servings: 4

Mediterranean Salad With Feta And Black Olives

1. Wash and dry greens using a salad spinner
2. Chop Romaine and Spinach and place in a large bowl
3. Slice onions thin
4. Cut fresh mint into very fine pieces and sprinkle
5. Put olive halves all around the bowl
6. Place tomato wedges in a decorative manner
7. Gently spread feta cheese throughout the bowl
8. Pour Dressing mixture all around and mix

Ingredients:

1/2 Purple Onion, sliced thin
1/2 Head Romaine lettuce
1 5 oz Package of baby spinach
7 Leaves of fresh mint
1 Can whole black olives,
      sliced in halves
1 6 oz cherry tomatoes,
      sliced in halves
1/2 Pound Feta cheese, cubed

Dressing:
Juice of one lemon
Black Pepper to taste
1 Tsp Pink Himalayan salt
2 Tbs Olive Oil

Servings: 6

Shutterstock / Barbara Dudzinska

Salad Nicoise

Dressing:
1. Place all the ingredients in a food processor
2. Blend until smooth
3. Pour into a glass airtight jar
4. Place in refrigerator
5. Reserve 2 anchovies to garnish the top of salad
6. This dressing will keep well in a glass jar stored in the refrigerator for a week.

Salad:
1. Wash, dry in a lettuce spinner and cut romaine lettuce into small slices
2. Place in a large bowl
3. Rinse and dry greens in a salad spinner and place over romaine
4. Slice cherry tomatoes into halves and spread on top of greens
5. Drain and place pieces of tuna evenly on top
6. Cut string beans into 1 inch sticks and place on top
7. Cut roasted peppers into thin slices, and place evenly
8. Place thin strips of red onion on top
9. Cut hard boiled eggs into 1/8 wedges and place evenly around
10. Slice radishes into very thin circles and spread on top
11. Drop olives evenly around
12. Place any leftover pieces of anchovies to garnish on top
13. Chop scallions into small slices to garnish
14. Pour dressing over generously

Ingredients:

Dressing:
8 Anchovies, boneless
4 Tbs capers
1 Bunch flat leaf parsley
2 3/4 Tbs Dijon mustard
5 Garlic cloves
3/4 Cup olive oil
1/4 Cup apple cider vinegar
1 1/2 Tbs oregeno
1 Tsp sea salt
1 Tsp black pepper

Salad:
1 Head romaine lettuce
1 12 Oz Bag mixed greens
2 Roasted red bell peppers, sliced thin
25 Small nicoise olives
4 Cans tuna or 1 1/4 pounds
4 Hard boiled eggs, cut into 1/8
4 Radishes, sliced thin
16 Cherry tomatoes
1/4 Red onion, cut into thin slivers
1/4 Pound steamed string beans
2 Scallions, chopped small

Servings: 8

Marinated Mozzarella Rolls

1. Slice Mozzarella into 12 thin slices 1 x 2 inches in length
2. Place slices in a large rectangle tupperware or tray. Set aside
3. In a small bowl, mix together 1/4 cup olive oil, chopped oregano, chopped chives, lemon juice, salt, pepper, vinegar, and tamari
4. Pour marinade over sliced mozzarella, cover and place in refrigerator for a minimum of 3 hours
5. Wash, dry and slice zucchini using a mandolin into 12 slices lengthwise
6. Heat a skillet with a drizzle of olive oil on medium-high heat
7. Carefully sear each side of the zucchini, about 10 seconds on each side, sprinkling salt and pepper over each slice, and set aside
8. Wash and cut plum tomatoes in half, removing the ends
9. Wash, separate and cut ends off of scallions, leaving them long
10. Using a cutting board or clean surface create 12 rolls, starting with the zucchini, the mozzarella on top, a leaf or two of basil, and half a plum tomato on top
11. Roll together and tie with a scallion strip
12. Plate and drizzle with remaining juices from the marinade
13. Serve garnished with extra basil leaves

Ingredients:

1 Bunch fresh basil leaves, washed and dried well
1 1/2 lb fresh mozzarella,
1/2 Cup olive oil
1/4 Cup fresh chives, chopped
3 Tbs fresh oregano, chopped
3 Tbs fresh lemon juice
4 Zucchini sliced thin, using a mandolin
6 Small ripe plum tomatoes
4 Bunches of scallions
1 Tsp sea salt
1 Tsp fresh ground black pepper
1 Tbs apple cider vinegar
1/2 Tsp gluten free tamari

Servings: 12

Shutterstock / Karl Allgaeuer

Stuffed Mushrooms

1. Preheat oven to 375
2. Prepare a large tray with parchment paper, greased well
3. Cut stems off mushrooms, and place in food processor
4. Add beef, scallions, oil, garlic, egg, parsley, flour, pepper & salt and pulse until becomes a fine meal texture
5. Fill each mushroom cap
6. Bake between 35-45 minutes until begins to look golden

Ingredients:

24 Medium portabella mushrooms
1/2 Pound beef
5 Scallions, finely sliced
7 Garlic cloves, minced
1/4 Cup coconut flour
1/4 Cup chopped fresh parsley
1 Large egg
1 Tsp Sea salt
3/4 Tsp black pepper
4 Tbs olive oil

Servings: 8 Dinner servings or 24 Appetizer servings

Creepy Crawly Spider Deviled Eggs

1. Boil eggs and run under cold water for two minutes
2. Peel and rinse eggs
3. Cut eggs in half lengthwise, remove yolks
4. Using a fork press down on the egg yolks to mash down
5. Stir in mayonnaise, mustard, salt, and pepper and press down to remove any big clumps
6. Cut whole olives in half
7. Sprinkle paprika all around the tops of the eggs
8. Put one half of the olive on top of the mashed yolk for the spiders body
9. Slice the other half for the spiders legs in 8 parts
10. Put four legs on each side

Ingredients:

1 Tsp Paprika
1/4 Tsp black pepper
1/8 tsp Pink Himalayan Salt
6 hard-boiled eggs, cut in half
3 Tbs Primal Kitchen mayo
3/4 Tsp Deli mustard
Pitted black olives

Servings: 6-12

Authentic Guacamole

1. Place avocados in food processor
2. Pulse until mostly smooth
3. Add all remaining ingredients to the food processor and pulse
4. Pulse 3 times just to combine, not mush
5. Serve garnished with a sprig of cilantro or a slice of lime

Ingredients:

1 Tomatillo
4 Ripe avocados
1/4 Cup minced red onion
1/4 sp ground black pepper
1/2 Tsp sea salt
Juice of 1 lime
3 Tbs diced tomatoes
2 Tbs Fresh cilantro
4 Cloves garlic
1 Jalapeno pepper, seeded

Servings: 6

Delicious!

Seared Tuna & Avocado Tartare

1. Heat up a small heavy skillet to medium high heat
2. Rub tuna with 3/4 Tbs olive oil
3. Sprinkle with a pinch of salt & pepper
4. Place in skillet and sear on each side to a golden color
5. Some like their fish cooked through while others prefer it rare
6. Please cook for at least a few minutes on each side if you would like it cooked thoroughly
7. Allow to cool
8. Using a cutting board chop tuna into small pieces
9. Add remaining ingredients and transfer to a bowl and toss until juices are all well absorbed
10. Serve chilled

Ingredients:

8 Ounces fresh tuna
4 Tbs extra virgin olive oil
1 Tsp sea salt
1/2 Tsp Pepper
1 Large avocado diced finely
1/3 Cup red onion, chopped finely
1/3 Cup fresh cilantro, chopped finely
1/4 Cup fresh squeezed lime juice
1 Chili pepper finely minced
Serve with lime wedges on the side

Servings: 4

Shutterstock / ajcabeza

CompletelyKeto

Soups & Stews

Creamy Turkey Soup

1. Using a pot big enough for a soup, sauté all vegetables in the basil, garlic, rosemary in oil until lightly golden
2. Add turkey and broth
3. Simmer for 20 minutes
4. Reduce heat to low and add almond milk, salt and pepper
5. Simmer 30 minutes
6. Remove from heat and serve garnished with finely chopped basil

Ingredients:

6 Cups chopped cooked turkey
2 Onions, chopped
2 Cups celery, chopped
4 Cups cauliflower, finely chopped
2 Cups fresh mushrooms, chopped
2 Tsps fresh basil, finely chopped
1 Tsp rosemary
2 Garlic cloves, smashed
4 Tsps coconut oil
6 Cups chicken broth
2 Cups unsweetened almond milk
1 1/2 Tsps kosher salt
1 Tsp black pepper

Servings: 14-16

Chili

1. Heat oil in a large pot
2. Mix together garlic, onion, red pepper, cilantro, parsley and celery in a food processor and just pulse until coarsely chopped
3. Add vegetable mix to hot oil in pot and saute until liquid has cooked off and is translucent, about 4 minutes
4. Add the tomatoes, wine, ground beef, chili powder, oregano, cumin, Swerve Sweetener, water, salt and pepper
5. Bring mixture to a boil and transfer to Crock Pot
6. Set Crock Pot to medium-low and cook, covered, for a minimum of 3 hours. The chili will be thin but thicker than a soup
7. Serve hot

Ingredients:

2 Pounds ground beef
2 Cups Pinot Noir
1/3 Cup olive oil
8 Cloves garlic
1 Large onion chopped
1 Large red bell pepper, seeded and cubed
1 Small bunch cilantro
1 Large bunch flat-leaf parsley
3 Celery stalks, peeled and cut
One 28-ounce can crushed tomatoes
1/4 Cup chili powder
2 Tbs oregeno
2 Tbs cumin
3 Tbs Swerve Granular
8 Cups water
1 Tsp Pink Himalayan Salt
1/2 Tsp ground black pepper

Servings: 8

Shutterstock / Shebeko

Instant Chicken Soup

1. Place all ingredients in Instant Pot
2. Set on pressure cook and lock
3. Follow instructions for soup on your cooker
4. Typically, it's 15 - 20 minutes cooking time

Ingredients:

1 Large onion, diced
3 pounds chicken legs & thighs
1 Tbs Pink Himalayan salt
1 Tsp Pepper
4 cloves of garlic, diced
3 baby carrots, for flavor only
1 parsnip, for flavor only
1/2 rutabaga, for flavor only
3 stalks of celery, small chunks
Sprig of parsley to garnish
2 1/2 quarts of water

Servings: 14

Thai Coconut Curry Soup

1. Drain the coconut and add meat to a high powered blender (give liquid to a non keto family member)
2. Add all remaining ingredients and blend on high
3. Chill in refrigerator for at least a couple of hours before serving
4. Mix well before serving
5. Garnish with Chili, red pepper, sliced Cilantro or basil leaves

Ingredients:

2 Young coconuts, meat only
2 Tomatoes
4 Tbs fresh cilantro
1 Tsp cayenne pepper
2 Tsp curry powder
1/2 Tsp Pink Himalayan Salt
8 Garlic cloves
6 Tbs lime juice
4 Tsp fresh ginger, minced
4 Tsp cold pressed olive oil

Servings: 4

Chicken Vegetable Soup

1. Using a large pot, boil water almost at 3/4 level of the pot
2. Add chicken
3. After it boils, skim the fat at the top. If you are using boneless chicken, there won't be much
4. Combine all of the vegetables, salt, and pepper and allow to come to a rolling boil
5. Keep on medium heat for 5 minutes and then simmer on low-medium heat for about two hours, covered

Ingredients:

4 Pieces of boneless chicken
    breast or bone-in
    legs and thighs
1 Whole tomato, peeled
3 Parsnips, peeled and cut up
1- 6 Oz Package of portabella mushrooms
1 Large onion, peeled
3 large zuchini
4 Stalks of celery, chopped
2 Carrots, peeled and chopped
1 Tbs Pink Himalayan Salt
1/2 Tsp ground black pepper

Helpful Hint:

Try the Completely Keto Matzo Balls with this soup for a satisfying meal! (Page 33)

Servings: 5

Goblin Soup

1. Grind the coriander, cumin, peppercorns, and salt with a hand herb grinder
2. Add other ingredients and combine into a paste texture
3. Using a blender mix 6 Tbs curry paste, spinach, and 1 cup coconut milk and set aside
4. In a large stockpot bring all remaining coconut milk to a slow boil
5. Reduce heat, stir in the curry spinach mixture and simmer for 5 minutes
6. Return to a medium-high temperature
7. Add zucchini and cook for 5 minutes
8. Add chicken and season with salt and pepper
9. Cook 5 minutes
10. Add basil
11. Garnish with serrano chiles

Ingredients:

Curry paste:
2 Tbs fresh lime juice
4 Scallions, diced very small
4 Serrano chiles, thinly sliced
Lime zest from two limes
2 1/2 Tbs fresh ginger, peeled and chopped
10 Garlic cloves, minced
3/4 Cup fresh cilantro
1 Tsp Coarse salt
2 1/2 Tsp whole cumin seeds
3 Stalks fresh lemongrass, chopped
1 1/2 Tsps whole black peppercorns, toasted
1 1/2 Tbs whole coriander seeds, toasted

Soup:
Serrano chiles for garnish
1 Cup fresh basil
25 Ounces boneless, skinless chicken, shredded
2 Zucchini sliced
30 Oz. unsweetened coconut milk
3 Ounces Spinach
Salt and Ground Pepper to taste

Servings: 8 - 10

Shutterstock / Nayoka

Chicken Soup

1. Use 12-16 Quart pot
2. Put everything in the pot and bring water level 1 inch from the top
3. Bring to a boil all together for about 10 minutes.
4. Skim the top of the soup
5. Continue to boil on low covered for 30 minutes
6. Skim the top of the soup a second time
7. Cook for another hour and then skim a third time
8. Simmer on low heat for a minimum of 90 minutes
9. Add Dill and continue to simmer for 15 minutes

Ingredients:

4 Stalks of celery, chunked
2 Carrots, cut into chunks
2 Garlic cloves, peeled
1 Whole onion, peeled
2 Parsnips, cut into chunks
1 Whole leek, cut up
2 Sprigs of fresh dill, chopped
8 chicken bottoms
1 Tsp Himalayan salt
1 Tsp black pepper
1 Tsp tumeric

Servings: 12 - 16

Helpful Hint:

Try the Completely Keto Matzo Balls with this soup for a satisfying meal! (Page 33)

Fish Stew

1. Place all ingredients in Instant Pot starting with all of the vegetables and spices, olive oil and olives stirring the flavors all together at first, and then add the fish and mixing gently with a wooden spoon or spatula.
2. Cook for 15 minutes using an Instant Pot on Quick/ Pressure Cook mode
3. Serve hot garnished with cilantro

Helpful Hints:

Choose fish that is readily available at your local fish market. Keep in mind the fish we recommend are thick and are less likely to fall apart than flounder or sole.

When preparing these ingredients please keep in mind that the chard reduces in volume in a matter of minutes. So don't worry if your Instant Pot looks too full.

Ingredients:

3 Pounds skinless, boneless
    sea bass, halibut, mahi
    mahi, grouper,
    or ocean perch
2 Cups water
2 Tbs Paprika
1 1/2 Tsps Tumeric
1/2 Cup Olive oil
30 Pitted green olives
3 Cups diced tomatoes
1 Head fennel, sliced very thin
10 Cloves garlic minced
2 Large bunches swiss chard,
    red or green, cut into
    1 inch strips, stems
    included

Servings: 8

Asparagus Soup

1. Gather the asparagus and place on a cutting board
2. Cut off the bottom part of each stalk of asparagus, and wash thoroughly
3. Chop up the rest of the asparagus leaving half of the flower end tips whole
4. Use a large deep skillet and put coconut oil on the bottom of the pan
5. Put on medium-high heat
6. Let heat up and place the asparagus and tarragon spice and cook on high tossing every minute or so
7. After ten minutes, remove half of the flower ends and put in a bowl on the side
8. Pour chicken stock in the pot
9. Add salt and pepper
10. Bring to a boil
11. Reduce heat to low until asparagus looks soft, about ten minutes
12. Using an immersion blender, blend until creamy
13. Serve individual bowls with a few pieces of Asparagus on top and perhaps a fresh green leaf for decorative purposes

Ingredients:

8 cups chicken broth
1 Tsp tarragon
3 Pounds thin asparagus
4 Tbs Coconut oil
1/2 Tsp black pepper
1 Tsp Pink Himalayan Salt

Servings: 8

Shutterstock / gkrphoto

Gazpacho Soup

1. Using a blender mix together the tomato juice, oil, and vinegar
2. Chop vegetables into chunks and blend
3. Add the garlic, salt, and pepper
4. Blend until vegetables are chopped finely
5. Chill for at least 3 hours
6. Soup can be prepared a couple days in advance of serving
7. This chilled soup can be garnished with:
   Cubed avocado
   Chopped cucumber
   Peppers
   Tomatoes
   Hard boiled eggs
   Diced scallions
   Parsley or Cilantro

Ingredients:

1/2 Green pepper
1/2 Cucumber, peeled
1 Tomato, peeled
1/2 Onion
2 Cloves garlic minced
1/4 Tsp Pink Himalayan Salt
Pinch black pepper
1 16 Ounce can tomato juice
1/4 Cup Olive oil
2 Tbsp Apple cider vinegar

Servings: 4

Light & Refreshing!

Shutterstock / Melinda Fawver

Simple Vegetable Soup

All vegetables have carbs. It's a fact. Keto means eliminating high insulin spiking veggies like potatoes, sweet potatoes, and rutabagas and focusing on lower carb veggies. If you want vegetable soup, it's going to need some flavors.
You can choose to enjoy the broth only from this soup and give the veggies to a non-keto member of your family. My 91 year old mom comes to mind…Or you can take care to divide up the veggies evenly into portions and track them in your daily macros. Yes, you are reading this recipe correctly. It has carrots, pumpkin, and turnips in them. However, this recipe serves 8. That brings the carb count way down. Enjoy.

1. Saute onions in olive oil and turmeric for 5 minutes.
2. Add carrots and saute for another 5 minutes.
3. Add 3 quarts of water, then vegetables and salt.
4. Cook for 1/2 an hour, then at the end add the fresh coriander and cook 5 more minutes.

Ingredients:

4 Tbs olive oil
1/4 tsp turmeric
6 smalls onions, peeled halved
1 carrot, peeled and chunked
2 turnip, peeled and chunked
1/2 cabbage, shredded
Whole medium pumpkin,
      chunked (remove skin)
1/2 bunch of fresh coriander,
      chopped
2 tsp Himalayan salt

Servings: 8

Matzo Balls

1. Beat eggs with Salt and Pepper for about a minute
2. Mix in the Almond flour and place in freezer for 30 minutes
3. Bring water or chicken stock to a boil
4. Wet fingers with water and roll the batter into balls and then drop into the pot of boiling water
5. Set temperature to simmer for 20 minutes

Ingredients:

2 Cups Almond Flour
7 Cups Water or Chicken Stock
4 Eggs
2 Tsp Himalayan Salt
1/4 Tsp Black Pepper

Servings: 10

Beef Stew

1. Using an Instant Pot set to Sauté mode setting:
2. Place beef in pot and brown beef for 3-5 minutes in the olive oil, remove and set on the side
3. Saute onion for 3 minutes stirring constantly and then add beef to insta pot and mix well
4. Add crushed garlic, tomato paste, whole portabella mushrooms, tomatoes, all spices and stir for a couple of minutes
5. Add kabocha squash, carrot, red pepper, and celery and stir again
6. Slowly pour in wine and Xanthan Gum and keep stirring
7. Add two cups or more of beef stock until liquid is covering over the beef
8. Turn off sauté mode and manually set timer for 20 minutes
9. Serve over a cup of cauliflower rice per serving

Ingredients:

3 Pounds stew beef,
    cut into 2 inch cubes
1 Tsp Xanthan Gum
1 1/2 Tsp onion powder
1 1/2 Tsp garlic powder
3 1/2 Tsp Pink Himalayan Salt
1 Tsp Paprika
5 Tbs Olive oil
1 Large Vidalia onion, cubed
7 Cloves garlic, crushed
2 Cups whole portabella
    mushrooms
1 1/2 Cups Kabocha squash ,
    cubed
1 Carrot, sliced thin
1 Red pepper, sliced into
    1 inch pieces
2 Tomatoes, diced
1 Tbs tomato paste
    (no sugar added)
2 Stalks celery, chopped small
2 Cups dry red wine
    (preferably Pinot Noir)
2 Cups beef stock
    (no sugar added)
1/4 Tsp curry powder
3 Tbs Wheat-free tamari
1 Tsp black pepper

Servings: 8

Creamy Zucchini Soup

1. Mix Ingredients. Easy peasy. Throw everything in a food processor or blender.
2. Pulse only. Do not liquify.
3. Add 1/2 teaspoon of xanthan gum. Pulse again.
4. Put into large pot and simmer for 40 minutes over low heat.
5. Stir from time to time.
6. Serve each portion with a piece of fresh basil.

Ingredients:

4 medium/large zucchini
    (wash but do not peel)
1 small diced onion
3 cups of water
    or vegetable broth
1 Tsp Himalayan salt
1/4 teaspoon freshly ground
    black pepper
1 1/2 Tbs tahini
1/2 Tsp cumin
1/2 Tsp dried basil
2 Tsp apple cider vinegar
1/2 Tsp lime juice
1/2 Tsp xanthan gum

Servings: 4

CompletelyKeto

Sandwiches & Burgers

Easy Beef Lettuce Wraps

1. Heat a deep pan over medium heat
2. Brown the beef, yellow onion and garlic until the beef is cooked through about 5-7 minutes
3. Place all beef seasoning mixture into a small bowl, mix well and add to meat
4. Add the Tomato puree and swerve and combine well
5. Place in a bowl and set aside
6. On a serving tray place lettuce around and spoon the cooked beef inside
7. Sprinkle on the chopped cilantro, cubed avocado, cucumber and red onion
8. Place lime wedges nearby in a small dish
9. At the time of serving squeeze lime on top generously

Ingredients:

3 Pounds ground beef
1/4 yellow onion, chopped
1 Cup no sugar tomato puree
1/2 Cup red onion, chopped
5 Cloves garlic, minced
2 Avocados, chopped into very small cubes
1 Bunch fresh cilantro, chopped
2 Limes, cut into 1/8 wedges
1 Cucumber, diced
1 Large romaine, butter or iceberg lettuce
1 Tsp swerve granular sweetener

Beef Seasoning:
1 1/2 Tbs chili powder
1 Tbs Pink Himalayan salt
3/4 Tbs Cumin
1/2 Tbs Oregano
1 Tsp onion powder
1 Tsp paprika
1/4 Tsp black pepper
1 Tsp cayenne pepper

Servings: 8

Fat Bomb Lettuce Wraps

1. Use a grinder made for coffee, nuts or spices and grind up 1 cup walnuts
2. Pour out the ground up walnuts from the grinder and roast in a small skillet on low
3. Add the salt
4. Stir around for about 3 minutes
5. Remove from skillet and allow to cool
6. Add 16 ounces of cream cheese to warm nuts
7. Sprinkle cinnamon and mix well
8. Refrigerate for 30 minutes
9. Remove from refrigerator
10. On a cutting board lay one leaf of lettuce at a time and spoon cream cheese and nut mixture inside in a log shape
11. Fold edges of lettuce in and fold underneath
12. Repeat again until mixture is finished
13. Place a toothpick in the center

Ingredients:

16 Ounces cream cheese
1/8 Tsp Pink Himalayan Salt
1/4 Tsp cinnamon
1 Cup walnuts
5 Oz butter lettuce

Servings: 16

Grilled Turkey Burger

1. In a large mixing bowl combine ground turkey with all ingredients except the olive oil
2. Divide the turkey into 6 equal portions and make patties and set aside
3. Heat up grill and then rub each turkey burger with olive oil on either side
4. Add burgers to heated up grill and cook well on each side 3-5 min
5. Serve with Fox Hill Kitchens Buns and Homemade Ketchup (page 156)
6. Add some fresh cilantro, parsley, tomato, cucumber or onion

Ingredients:

2 Pounds ground turkey
6 Fox Hill Kitchens Buns
1 Tbs lime juice
1 Tsp oregeno
1/4 Tsp cumin
1 Tsp fine sea salt
1/2 Tsp black pepper
1 Tsp garlic powder
1 Tbs olive oil

Servings: 6

Tuna Sliders

1. Using a food processor pulse 5 times the tuna meat into a fine ground tuna
2. Transfer ground tuna to a large bowl and combine mustard, olive oil, all spices, scallions, garlic, and Wheat-free tamari
3. Shape into 6 slider-sized patties
4. Cover and store in the refrigerator at least 2 hours in advance
5. To make the Mustard Dressing, mix all ingredients together, place in a small container and refrigerate
6. Coat a grill pan with oil and heat until very hot
7. Add sliders and cook for around 2 minutes per side
8. Assemble sliders with: small buns, a layer or two of lettuce, spring greens, tomato slices, and avocado slices
9. Pour mustard dressing over the top of veggies and tuna slider and close top of bun

Ingredients:

3/4 Pound Sashimi-grade tuna
1/2 Tbs dijon mustard
1/2 Tbs olive oil
1/4 Tsp paprika
1/4 Tsp black pepper
1 Tsp kosher salt
1/4 Tsp red pepper
1/4 Tsp garlic powder
2 Scallions, finely chopped
2 Small garlic cloves, minced
1/2 Tbs Wheat-free tamari
1/2 Tbs fresh ground ginger

Assembly:
Fox Hill Kitchens Small Buns
1 Small head of butter lettuce
Bunch of spring greens
1 Large tomato, sliced
1 Avocado, sliced thin

Mustard dressing:
2 Tbs dijon mustard
1 Tsp lime juice
2 Tbs Primal Kitchen Mayo
1/4 Tsp Cayenne pepper
2 Tsp water
1 Tsp Pink Himalayan Salt

Servings: 2

Shutterstock / gorillaimages

Salmon Burgers With Thai Sweet Chili Sauce

1. Clean the fillet, removing the skin and bones but leaving the fat
2. Fry the white side of the fish in a small amount of oil or butter until golden and set aside
3. Chop up the scallions and red pepper and fry in the same pan as the fish and set aside
4. Cut up 1/3 of the fish into very small cubes
5. Grind the rest of the fish in a food processor with the fried scallions and red pepper, ginger, and Wheat-free tamari
6. Transfer to a large bowl and combine the cubed fish and ground up fish mixture
7. Wet hands and shape into medium-sized patties
8. Cover tightly with plastic wrap and refrigerate for a minimum of two hours
9. Using a large non-stick skillet, fry the salmon burgers in oil or butter on medium heat
10. Do not turn over until seared on one side
11. Lower heat to a low setting, fry the other side until golden
12. Serve with guacamole and homemade Thai sweet chili sauce and garnish with some basil greens

Thai Sweet Chili Sauce:

1. In a food processor blend together all ingredients except for the Xanthan Gum and 2 tablespoons of water to be mixed together and set on the side
2. Puree the mixture until smooth
3. Transfer to a small pan, bring to a boil, and then simmer for about 2-3 minutes
4. Add the Xanthan Gum and 2 tablespoons water to the pan and mix well
5. Bring to a boil for 1 minute
6. Remove from pan and allow to cool in refrigerator before serving on the side with the Salmon Burgers

Ingredients:

2 1/2 Pounds salmon fillet
1 Bunch scallions
1 Tsp grated ginger
1/2 Red pepper, finely diced
4 Tbs Wheat-free tamari
Olive oil or butter for frying

Thai Sweet Chili Sauce:
3 Garlic cloves
2 Hot red peppers
3/4 Cup water
1/2 Tsp Pink Himalayan salt
1/2 Cup Swerve granular
1/4 Cup apple cider vinegar
1/4 Tsp Xanthan Gum

Servings: 6-8

Easy 3-Ingredient Cheese Sandwich

1. Wash lettuce thoroughly and put in a Salad Spinner
2. Place two pieces of lettuce cut in halves on one part of the plate, do that two more times by creating 3 small lettuce beds with 4 halves in each
3. Spoon 2 Oz Farmer cheese onto each lettuce bed and top with a nice slice of tomato
4. You can add any spice if you want. These 3 Ingredients alone are very tasty!

Ingredients:

6 Oz Farmer Cheese
3 Slices Tomato
6 Slices Romaine Lettuce

Servings: 1

Helpful Hint:

It's easy to wash a whole head of lettuce and then remove the water and keep it crisp by using a Salad Spinner. You can store it in an airtight container or large ziploc bag for up to 3 days. This is an easy and practical way to have the lettuce ready-to-go as a sandwich builder.

Bagel, Lox and Cream Cheese

Whether you have friends over or just want to wake up to something delicious and quick to indulge in by yourself, there is nothing like a fresh bagel and lox! I order keto-friendly bagels from Fox Hill Kitchens and have them delivered to my door.

1. Toast bagel lightly
2. Smear cream cheese evenly
3. Slice tomato
4. Slice red onion thinly (optional)
5. Use a Smoked Salmon that is high in quality and has no sugar
6. Squeeze some fresh lemon on your lox and sprinkle some capers all over

Ingredients:

4 Fox Hill bagels
4 oz. cream cheese
1 tomato
1 red onion
4 oz. smoked salmon
lemon and capers (optional)

Servings: 4

Shutterstock / Alena Haurylik

Spinach And Toasted Pecans Hamburger

1. In a large pot quickly blanch spinach for one minute in boiling water and a pinch of salt
2. Drain and cool
3. Squeeze the spinach until it is firm and dry and chop very small
4. In a pan, fry onions chopped up into very small squares and drain on paper towels as it cools
5. In a large mixing bowl place beef, spinach, black pepper, salt, vodka, coconut oil, minced garlic, fried onions, and seltzer
6. Knead well together
7. Toast pecans in a fry pan, chop small and add to meat mixture and mix
8. Cover and place in fridge for a minimum of 2 hours
9. Shape hamburger patties
10. Grill the hamburgers on an Indoor Barbecue to desired doneness

Ingredients:

2 1/2 Pounds fresh ground beef
1 Tsp Coarse ground black pepper
2 Large onion
1/2 Cup olive oil for frying
5 Oz Toasted pecans
1 Tbs coconut oil
1 Tsp Kosher salt
1 Tsp Minced garlic
25 Oz Washed spinach
2 Tbs Vodka
1 Cup seltzer

Servings: 6-8

You can choose to prepare your burger and serve on a bed of lettuce, with cut up avocado slices, tomatoes, peppers and green beans or any side you chose or you can serve on a hamburger bun from Fox Hill Kitchens.

Shutterstock / Brent Hofacker

Tuna Melt On A Log

1. Preheat oven to 350
2. Cut zucchini in half lengthwise
3. Remove all seeds carefully not to break the zucchini using a small spoon or melon scooper
4. Grease oven safe pan with butter
5. Place zucchini halves into the pan open side up
6. Bake for 20 minutes
7. In a medium sized bowl add tuna or salmon, celery salt, black pepper, cheddar cheese, garlic and mayo & mix well
8. Remove zucchini from oven and spoon tuna or salmon mix into the logs
9. Sprinkle mozzarella cheese over each log
10. Bake in oven 15 minutes or until golden
11. Remove from oven and sprinkle parmesan cheese over
12. Garnish with parsley
13. Serve with cherry tomatoes on the side

Ingredients:

3 Medium zucchini
2 Garlic cloves, minced
3 5 Oz Cans tuna or salmon
2 Tbs Primal Kitchen Mayonnaise
2 Tsp celery salt
Black pepper to taste
6 Oz shredded Mozzarella cheese
2 Oz Parmesan cheese
2 Oz shredded Cheddar cheese
2 Tbs butter
Garnish with fresh parsley and cherry tomatoes

Servings: 6

Turkey Zucchini Burgers

1. Place all ingredients in a large bowl (except for the coconut oil).
2. Preheat your oven to 400 degrees
3. Shape your burgers into small patties.
4. You should get about 16 small patties out of this mixture
5. Sear the burgers in the coconut oil on each side until they are golden brown
6. Put them on a cookie sheet with parchment paper.
7. Bake in your oven for 7-8 minutes.
8. Serve topped with parsley or tahini sauce for a Middle Eastern flavor

Ingredients:

1 pound of ground turkey
1 large zucchini, ground
2 scallions, sliced thin
1 egg
2 tablespoons mint, chopped
2 cloves of garlic, minced finely
1 tablespoon of ground cumin
1 teaspoon pink Himalayan salt
1/2 tablespoon of black pepper
1/2 tablespoon of hot pepper
Coconut oil for cooking

Servings: 16

Shutterstock / SosnaRadosna

Main Dishes

Chicken Bolognese Sauce & Angel Hair Zoodles

1. Using a Spiralizer, create angel hair pasta with zucchini and set aside in a bowl
2. Using a skillet, sauté onion in 1 tablespoon of olive oil until golden and set aside
3. In a heavy large saucepan set on medium-high heat, brown ground chicken in 2 tablespoons of olive oil, stirring constantly for about 3-6 minutes until cooked through
4. Add cooked onion to chicken and stir on low-medium heat
5. In a skillet, sauté chopped tomatoes in 1 tablespoon of olive oil for 2 minutes and then add to pot with chicken and onion mixture
6. Pour tomato paste, water, and swerve into the pot and mix
7. Add cilantro, garlic powder, paprika, salt, and black pepper and combine then reduce to low and cover for 20 minutes
8. Serve hot over your angel hair zoodles

Ingredients:

3 Pounds ground chicken
8 Small zucchini made into angel hair zoodles
1 Large onion, cubed
2 Large tomatoes, chopped
1 Bunch cilantro, chopped finely
2 Small cans (no sugar added) tomato paste
1 1/2 cups water
1 Tbs garlic powder
1 1/2 Tbs Paprika
1 Tsp black pepper
2 Tsp Sea salt
4 Tbs Olive oil
1 1/2 Tbs Swerve

Servings: 8 - 10

Chinese Lemon Chicken

1. In a large bowl toss together the chicken pieces, Wheat-free tamari and 1 tablespoon Agar Agar and cover, set aside to marinate for 30 minutes
2. In a small bowl mix lemon juice, Swerve Sweetener, water, lemon zest and 1 tablespoon Agar Agar and set aside
3. Mixing well to coat each piece of chicken, add almond flour, and remaining Agar Agar to the large bowl with the chicken marinating
4. In a frying pan with oil at least 2 1/2 inches deep, using a thermometer heat up oil to 350 degrees
5. Fry chicken pieces in very small batches to allow even cooking and no sticking during the cooking process
6. Cook until golden
7. Transfer pieces as they are done to a heavy skillet
8. Turn the heat to medium high on the skillet when finished frying all of the pieces, and pour the lemon zest sauce over chicken and toss
9. Cook for just a few seconds until sauce thickens

Ingredients:

1 lb dark chicken cut into pieces
1 Tbs Wheat-free tamari
1/2 Cup water
1/3 Cup fresh lemon juice
3 Tbs Swerve Granular
1 Tsp lemon zest
1/4 Cup Super Fine Almond
    flour
1/4 Cup Agar Agar
Avocado or coconut oil
    for frying

Servings: 6

Air Fryer Whole Roast Chicken

This recipe gives you a flavorful, crispy on the outside yet moist on the inside, quick and easy meal with a minimal amount of prep time! Enjoy!

1. Clean and dry chicken by patting with paper towels
2. Rub entire chicken with olive oil
3. Combine all spices and salt to create a dry rub
4. Sprinkle dry rub mix on chicken
5. Spray Air Fryer basket with a cooking spray and place the chicken into the basket with the legs down
6. Roast chicken for 30 minutes on 335 degrees
7. Flip chicken
8. Roast for 20 more minutes
9. Chicken should be golden in color and ready to eat

Ingredients:

1 3-5 pound whole chicken
1 Tbs light olive oil

Rub mixture:
1 Tsp black pepper
1/2 Tsp Kosher salt
1 Tbs paprika
1 Tbs garlic powder
1 Tsp parsley flakes

Servings: 8

Shutterstock / Africa Studio

Schnitzel

1. Using a large bowl combine eggs, mustard, salt, and pepper and mix
2. Toss chicken breasts inside the mix and let sit for a few minutes
3. Using a large flat plate with the almond meal, dip one piece of chicken at a time on each side
4. Heat up oil in fryer
5. Place in the fryer until lightly golden
6. Serve on a bed of greens or a fresh salad

Ingredients:

Avocado, Olive, or Coconut oil for frying

16 Thin slices of boneless chicken breast

4 Eggs

1 Tsp salt

1/4 Tsp black pepper

4-6 cups Almond Meal

1 Tbs of deli mustard

Servings: 6 - 8

Shawarma and Bok Choy

1. Boil chicken breast in water on high flame for 15-20 minutes letting it cook until fluffy
2. Remove and cut into thin slices no bigger than finger size
3. Set aside
4. Cut your onions in long strips
5. Use a pan minimum 2 inches deep
6. Heat pan
7. Add a little oil on high flame
8. Add your onions, Sprinkle with salt to allow onions to start to caramelize
9. Add cut up chicken breast and put seasonings on top
10. Sauté on medium high flame for 7 minutes
11. Add 1/4 cup water and cook 10 minutes on low heat
12. While The Shawarma is cooking, steam bok choy
13. Serve with Shawarma on top of bok choy. Pairs well with an Israeli salad and Tehini sauce

Ingredients:

4 big bok choy or 6 small
2 big onions or 4 small onions
4 pieces chicken breast
Seasoning:
1 Tbsp Olive oil
1 Tsp Pink Himalayan salt
2 mounted Tsp of paprika
Sprinkle of black pepper

Servings: 2 - 4

Southern Fried Chicken

1. Gently mix all ingredients together to form batter
2. Dip chicken piece by piece in the batter
3. Add chicken to Air Fryer
4. Set timer for 20 minutes. Wings, legs, and thighs will be done. Breast may need a little more time. If so, turn and add 10 minutes

Ingredients:

1 Whole chicken, cut into 1/8
3 eggs
1 tablespoon of water
1 teaspoon garlic powder
1 teaspoon of white pepper
3/4 cup almond flour
2 teaspoons of Himalayan salt
Pinch Black Pepper
1 tablespoon of hot paprika

Servings: 4 - 6

Shutterstock / George W. Bailey

Sweet Chicken and Jalapeño Slices

This recipe gives you a flavorful, crispy on the outside yet moist on the inside, quick and easy meal with a minimal amount of prep time! Enjoy!

1. Using an electric wok or one for the stovetop, sauté the jalapeño slices in the Lakanto syrup, minced garlic, and salt on medium heat
2. Add the small pieces of chicken breast with the temperature on medium-high heat stirring constantly for about ten minutes
3. Cook covered on low-medium heat for about 20 minutes
4. Chicken will be coated with the sweet and spicy sauce and look golden brown

Ingredients:

1/2 Cup Lakanto Syrup
3 Pounds boneless chicken breast, diced
3 Jalapeños, sliced thin
1 Tsp Pink Himalayan Salt
7 Garlic cloves, minced finely

Servings: 6

Sweet & Spicy!

Shutterstock / Jade Y

Mediterranean Chicken

1. Clean your chicken
2. Add chicken to Roasting Pan
3. Add seasoning then mix
4. Put aside to marinate
5. Preheat oven to 350 degrees
6. Dice onions
7. Cut lemon in slices
8. Cut celery into sticks, keeping them finger length
9. Chop cilantro
10. Place everything into the roasting pan with chicken and spices by adding everything together and mixing well
11. Add half a cup of water
12. Cover with aluminum foil
13. Let cook for 1 hour covered
14. Then uncover and cook for an additional 30 minutes
15. Depending on your oven make sure to check till golden brown

Ingredients:

5 legs and 5 Thighs or
       10 chicken breast fillets
2 big onions or 4 small
1 cup chopped cilantro
1 lemon
1 bunch of celery
1 cup pitted green olives
4 tbs olive oil
1 1/2 tsp Himalayan salt
2 tsp turmeric
Sprinkle black pepper

Servings: 10

Shutterstock / Liliya Kandrashevich

Simple Roast Chicken

1. Rub each piece of chicken with olive oil
2. Sprinkle each piece with paprika, garlic powder, black pepper, and a pinch of pink Himalayan salt
3. Bake it open in the oven at 350 degrees for 1 1/4 hours
4. The olive oil will make the skin crispy and golden and hold the spices in place

Easy & Delicious!

Ingredients:

1 whole chicken, quartered
olive oil
paprika
garlic powder
black pepper
pink Himalayan salt

Servings: 4 - 8

Shutterstock / Liv friis-larsen

Sweet & Sour Chicken

1. In a wok or frying pan add two tablespoons of olive oil or coconut oil and simmer minced ginger and onion for 5 minutes
2. Cut chicken cutlets into strips and add to pan
3. Simmer chicken for 5-8 minutes turning ocassionally
4. Cut up and add peppers to your pan
5. Add 3 tablespoons of Lakanto sweetener mixed with 1/2 teaspoon of xanthan gum
6. Add apple cider vinegar and water or chicken broth
7. Simmer for five minutes and stir
8. Serve over riced cauliflower with Wheat-free tamari

Ingredients:

Olive or coconut oil for frying
1 Tbs minced ginger
2 large chicken cutlets
1 red pepper
1 green pepper
1/2 yellow pepper
3 Tbs Lakanto
1/2 Tsp Xanthan gum
3 Tbs Apple cider vinegar
1/4 cup water or chicken broth

Servings: 4

Curry Chicken with Zucchini

1. Using a large heavy deep skillet, heat up the oil on high heat
2. In a food processor, coarsely chop the onion and jalapeño
3. Add the ground mixture to the hot oil and sauté
4. Add the curry and mustard seeds and stir for one minute
5. Add the water, chicken, and remaining ingredients and bring to a boil
6. Reduce to medium heat, cover, and cook for 1 hour
7. Watch to be sure that there is enough liquid in the pot, adding a little if necessary. The sauce should be thick
8. Serve hot

Ingredients:

3 Tbs Olive Oil
1 Large Onion, quartered
1 Jalapeño Pepper
3 Tbs Curry
1 Tbs Mustard Seeds
12 Pieces Chicken (drumsticks, thighs or thick cutlets)
2 Cups Water
2 Large Tomatoes, or 4 large plum tomatoes, seeded and diced
3 Large Zuchini, sliced in 1 inch circles

Servings: 6

Shutterstock /Murni

Chili Lime Chicken

1. Gently Mix all ingredients together
2. Add Mixture to Air Fryer
3. Set timer for 20 minutes
4. Try to save some for the rest of your family!

Ingredients:

1 Package of chicken legs, wings
    or drumettes
Trader Joe's Chili Lime Spice
Black Pepper to taste
Extra Virgin Olive Oil to cover

Servings: 4 - 8

Slow Cooker Salsa Chicken

1. Plug in slow cooker, set on high
2. Place chicken and all spices in a bowl, mix together and allow to sit and marinate well together for a few minutes
3. Pour spiced chicken in the slow cooker and pour salsa over the chicken
4. Pour 2 Cups of water on the bottom of slow cooker
5. Turn on low after water is steaming and hot
6. Allow to cook until looks tender or when you are ready to eat

Ingredients:

1 Jar 12-18 oz salsa of choice,
        No sugar added
2 Pounds skinless, boneless
        chicken breasts or thighs
6 Garlic cloves, minced
1/4 Tsp ground black pepper
1 Tsp sea salt
1 1/2 Tbs Chili powder
1 Tsp smokey paprika
1 Tsp garlic powder
1/2 Tsp oregeno
1 Tsp cumin
1 Tsp onion powder

Servings: 6

Hungarian Chicken Paprikash

1. Add olive oil to your Instant pot
2. Add onion and garlic and turn to Saute
3. Stir frequently for 3 minutes
4. Add all other ingredients and stir
5. Lock your instant pot and set it to automatic cook

Ingredients:

2 Large onions, diced
3 cloves of garlic, minced
1 chicken cut up in 1/8th
1 1/2 Tsp Pink Himalayan salt
2 Tsp Pepper
2 Tbs Sweet paprika
1 Tbs Smokey paprika
Jvuice of 1/2 lemon
1 tomato
1 Tbs tomato paste
1 bay leaf
3 Tbs olive oil
2 cups of chicken stock or water

Servings: 4 - 6

Shutterstock / Bartosz Luczak

Instant Barbecue Chicken

1. Turn your Instant Pot on Saute
2. All ingredients except for the chicken
3. Simmer the ingredients for 5 minutes then turn off.
4. Place the chicken on top of the sauce
5. Spoon the sauce on top of the chicken
6. Using your Instant pot on MANUAL, close the pot and seal it.
7. Cook on low pressure for 15 minutes.
8. Let the pressure release
9. Using a wooden slotted spoon take the chicken out and place it on a platter.
10. Turn the Instant Pot Back to Simmer and let it simmer for 5 more minutes
11. Sprinkle with white sesame seeds
12. Serve with sauce for dipping. (Save the extra sauce!)

Ingredients:

2 cups Sugar Free Tomato sauce
2 drops Sugar Free Liquid Smoke
2/3 cup Apple cider vinegar
1 tblsp Bourbon
2/3 cup Lakanto, Xylitol, or Swerve
2 tblsp coconut oil
1 tblsp prepared yellow mustard
1 Onion, medium, finely chopped
2 Garlic cloves, minced
2 Tbs Chili powder
1/2 tsp ground Black pepper
1/2 tsp cumin
1/2 tsp fresh oregano
1 leaf fresh basil, minced
1 tsp sugar free hot sauce
2 1/2 pounds skinless and boneless chicken thighs

Servings: 10

Overnight Marinated Rosemary Chicken

1. Cut chicken breasts in half lengthwise
2. In a food processor combine oil, salt, pepper, rosemary and lemon juice
3. Use a deep glass dish or tupperware container with a lid
4. Lay chicken pieces flat in deep dish or tupperware
5. Pour rosemary sauce over
6. Cover
7. Refrigerate overnight
8. Remove from refrigerator when ready to cook
9. Heat a skillet on medium-high
10. Cook two pieces of chicken at a time
11. Sear and cook on each side for about 4-5 minutes, or until golden and looks cooked through
12. Serve warm

Ingredients:

1 1/2 Pounds chicken breasts, boneless
2 Tsp fresh rosemary, ground in food processor
1/2 Cup olive oil
1/2 Cup lemon juice
1 1/2 Tsp sea salt
3/4 Tsp black pepper

Servings: 6

Shutterstock /Liliya Kandrashevich

Chicken Fried "Rice"

1. In a Wok heated to medium-high setting, add olive oil, chicken, garlic powder, and paprika
2. For about 5-7 minutes, toss and stir around with a spatula or large wooden spoon
3. Change setting to medium-low and continue to cook for 3-5 more minutes stirring occasionally
4. Remove chicken with a slotted spoon or spatula with holes and leave the juices from chicken in wok. Set chicken on the side in a bowl
5. In the wok, add scallions, carrot, and string beans for about 2-3 minutes while stirring
6. Remove from wok and set aside with chicken cubes
7. Place cauliflower rice in wok with minced garlic on medium-low and stir for about 2-4 minutes until lightly browned
8. Remove and set aside with the chicken and veggie mixture
9. Add beaten eggs to wok and scramble up for 2 minutes
10. Add the remaining ingredients that were set aside back into the wok and stir
11. Drizzle with Wheat-free tamari, salt and black pepper
12. Cook for about 2 minutes or so until well combined and chicken is heated

Ingredients:

16 Oz boneless skinless chicken breasts, diced
4 Tbs Light olive oil
1/4 Tsp garlic powder
1/4 Tsp paprika
1/4 Carrot, finely chopped
5 String beans, sliced thin
5 Scallions, chopped
4 Large garlic cloves, minced
3 Extra large eggs, beaten
4 Cups cauliflower rice
3 Tbs Wheat-free tamari
1 Tsp Pink Himalayan Salt
1/2 Tsp ground black pepper

Servings: 6

A Harlan Favorite!

Jamaican Jerk Chicken

1. Combine the onion, scallions, chili peppers, garlic, Jerk Spice, all spice, black pepper, nutmeg, thyme, and salt in your food processor
2. Keep processing until in turns into a semi-thick paste
3. While the machine is on, add the Wheat-free tamari and coconut oil
4. Pour the mixture into a large pyrex pan
5. Put the chicken in the pan and mix it up
6. Coat the chicken with the sauce
7. Cover and refrigerate overnight
8. Fire up your grill
9. With the grill set on high, score the meat on the grill until those gorgeous lines appear
10. Immediately lower the grill to medium
11. Cook with the grill closed to keep the spice mixture sharp
12. Use your thermometer to make sure the chicken is done
13. Garnish with slices of lemon or lime

Ingredients:

1 medium/large onion, chopped
3 scallions, chopped
2 chili peppers, chopped
3 garlic cloves, minced
1 Tbs ground allspice
1 Tbs black pepper
1 Tsp of ground thyme
1 Tsp Himalayan salt
1 Tsp ground nutmeg
1/2 cup Wheat-free tamari
1 Tbs Jamaican Jerk spice, ground
1 tablespoon coconut oil
2 whole chickens, cut in eighths

Servings: 8-10

Smoked Holiday Turkey

1. Soak pecan wood chips in a big bowl of cold water for a minimum of 6 hours and no more than 24 hours
2. Using either a smoker or charcoal grill
3. Set charcoal grill or smoker for indirect heat, to around 275 degrees
4. Add the soaked pecan wood chips to hot charcoal and allow them to char very well before starting to smoke the turkey
5. Place the turkey on a rack in a roasting pan
6. Brush entire turkey with oil generously, all around and on the sides using a food basting brush
7. Sprinkle the kosher salt and black pepper on turkey evenly
8. Place roaster pan in smoker or charcoal grill with the top shut completely closed for 45 minutes
9. In a bowl combine the vinegar, chicken stock, and Lakanto and baste the turkey every 45 minutes
10. Keep basting until, when using a Turkey thermometer the internal temperature of the part of the breast registers to 155 degrees and the internal temperature inside the thigh registers to 165 degrees
11. The turkey should be a very golden brown color and should be done between 3-5 hours
12. When it is ready you can remove the rack and pan and reserve juices for the gravy
13. Place turkey on a large cutting board and allow to cool down for 20 minutes before carving

Ingredients:

1 fresh whole turkey,
     14-18 pounds, lightly
     dried with paper towels
2 1/4 Tbs Apple Cider Vinegar
2 Tbs Lakanto Syrup Sweetener
1 1/2 Cups chicken stock
1 Tbs Kosher salt
2 Tsp fine ground black pepper
2 Tbs Avocado or coconut oil
Pecan wood chips for smoking

Servings: 14 - 20

Shutterstock / tdoes

Herbed Roasted Turkey

1. Preheat oven to 400
2. Using a large pot or plastic tub combine 1 gallon of water with kosher salt and the Swerve and lay turkey on it's breast side, so that it is resting in the brine
3. Refrigerate for 8 to 10 hours
4. Rinse Turkey in cool water and dry off with paper towels
5. Place half of the onion, carrot, and celery inside the cavity of the turkey
6. Using kitchen string, tie the turkey legs together
7. Place remaining celery, onion and carrot in the bottom of the turkey roasting pan
8. Place the turkey breast side up on a roasting rack in the pan
9. Brush the turkey with the mixture of the black pepper, paprika and parsley combined with the oil
10. Pour 2 1/2 cups of water into the pan and roast the turkey for 45 minutes
11. Baste the turkey and roast for another 1 1/2 hours, basting every 20 minutes
12. The turkey pan should be rotated each time you baste to ensure even roasting in your oven
13. The turkey is ready when using your poultry thermometer and it registers 165 degrees
14. Carve turkey on cutting board after cooling for 20 minutes

Ingredients:

One 13-15 Pound Turkey, rinsed
4 Tbs Olive oil
3 Celery ribs, chopped
1 Carrot, chopped
1 Large onion, chopped
1 1/2 Tsps ground black pepper
2 Tbs fresh flat leaf parsley
2 Tbs paprika
1 1/4 Cups Swerve Sweetener
1 1/4 Cups Kosher salt

Servings: 13 - 15

Turkey Boulette and Rice

1. In a pot of water, boil 1 head of celery cut into small slices for 10 minutes, drain, and set aside for the broth
2. In a large pot boil 3 cups water, 1/4 Cup olive oil, 2 Cloves garlic, 1/4 Tsp tumeric, 1/2 Tsp paprika
3. Prepare Miracle Rice as indicated on package and set aside
4. In a large bowl combine all ingredients in Boulette, mix together well and set aside
5. In a large pot mix all the broth ingredients, including the cooked celery and boil on medium for one minute
6. Using a bowl of water to moisten your fingers, carefully shape balls for the boulette and drop into boiling broth until you have completed the mixture.
7. Continue to boil on medium heat uncovered for 5 more minutes
8. Cover and cook on low-medium heat for an hour
9. Serve over Miracle Rice
10. Use the juices in the pan for gravy

Ingredients:

Boulette:
2 Pounds ground turkey
2 Tbs almond flour
1 Onion finely chopped
1/2 Cup chopped parsley
1 egg
3 Tbs olive oil
2 Tbs water
1/4 Tsp Pink Himalayan Salt
1/4 Tsp cinnamo
1/4 Tsp nutmeg
1/4 Tsp black pepper
1/4 Tsp ginger powder
1/4 Tsp white pepper
1/4 Tsp tumeric

Broth:
3 cups water
1/4 Cup olive oil
2 Cloves garlic
1/4 Tsp tumeric
1/2 Tsp paprika
1 Head of celery

Servings: 8 - 10

Bourbon and Lakanto Roast Turkey

1. In a large Poultry baking bag, place the Orange extract and water, Bourbon, Lakanto, thyme, 1-1/2 teaspoons of salt and 1-1/2 teaspoons of black pepper and mix well
2. Add the turkey to the bag and shake around the juices so that the turkey will be well marinated
3. Place in refrigerator overnight
4. Preheat oven to 325
5. Place Turkey in a large roasting pan and pour the juices into a bowl and set aside
6. Using 8 tablespoons of the oil, give a good rub to the entire turkey
7. Tie the legs together with kitchen string
8. Pour 1/2 cup of the set aside marinade into the roasting pan
9. Bake for 30 minutes
10. Baste the Turkey with the pan juices and add to the pan one cup of water
11. Bake the Turkey for 1 more hour, basting every 30 minutes
12. Add the remaining marinade to the pan
13. Cover the turkey all around loosely and cook for around two hours or until a poultry thermometer inserted in the thigh shows 165.
14. When turkey is golden and has reached desired temperature remove from oven and place on a platter and garnish with Rosemary sprigs.
15. Pour the gravy into a large gravy boat and serve hot alongside your Turkey platter.

Ingredients:

One 16-20 pound Turkey
4 Sprigs of Rosemary to garnish
4 Ounces Coconut oil
Ground Black Pepper
Pink Himalayan Salt
1 Tbs freshly chopped thyme
3 Tbs Orange Extract
         in 1/4 cup water
1/2 cup Lakanto Sweetener
1 1/2 Cups Bourbon

Servings: 16 - 20

Peking Duck

1. If you purchased frozen duck, defrost it in the refrigerator. Once the duck is completely defrosted, take it out of the refrigerator 30 minutes prior to cooking to bring it to room temperature
2. Preheat oven to 350
3. Remove the giblets from inside the duck. Rinse it, inside and outside, with cold water. Pat dry with paper towels
4. Set the duck on the working surface. Score the skin on the breast in a diamond pattern, making sure you only cut the skin, without reaching the meat. Poke the other fatty parts of the duck with the tip of the knife all over, to ensure fat release, especially in very fatty parts. You don't need to poke the legs as the skin is pretty thin there (except for where the legs connect to the body). Season very generously with salt both inside the cavity of the duck and outside on the skin, legs, all over. Place the duck breast side up
5. Mix all spices together. Sprinkle the top of the duck with the spice mix and put one teaspoon inside the cavity. Put chopped garlic cloves and lemon slices inside the duck cavity. The duck will have flapping skin on both ends - fold that skin inwards, to hold the garlic and lemon inside. Tie up the legs with butcher's twine
6. Place the bird breast side up on a large roasting pan with a rack (roasting pan should have a roasting rack to lift the duck from the bottom of the pan and allow the fat to drip below the duck). Roast the duck, breast side up, for 1 hour at 350 F
7. After 1 hour of roasting, flip the duck on its breast and roast it breast side down for 40 minutes, at 350 F
8. Remove the roasting pan with the duck from the oven and carefully pour off all the duck fat juices from the roasting pan into a large container
9. Flip the duck breast side up again on a rack in a roasting pan. Brush all of the duck with the freshly squeezed juice of 1 lemon, tamari, and Lakanto. (especially the scored duck breast) and cook the duck breast side up for another 40 minutes at 350 F, brushing every 10 minutes with the mixture
10. Roast for another 40 minutes. You can even carefully broil the duck for the last 10-15 minutes if you like (do it carefully, checking the duck regularly to make sure it doesn't char too much)v
11. After the duck is cooked, remove it from the oven, let stand for 15 minutes. Then, remove and discard the lemon from the cavity. Carve and serve!

Ingredients:

1 whole 4-6 lb duck
½ Tsp ground cinnamon
½ Tsp ground fresh ginger
¼ Tsp ground nutmeg
¼ Tsp ground white pepper
3 Tbs Wheat free tamari
1 Tbs Lakanto syrup
Salt to taste
5 garlic cloves, chopped
1 lemon, small or medium sliced
1 lemon, freshly squeezed juice

Servings: 6

Fried Fish

1. In a bowl mix together fish fillets with beaten egg and set aside
2. In a separate large plate combine almond flour, coconut flour, salt & spices
3. Take one fillet of fish at a time and coat well on both sides with the flour mixture and set aside
4. Heat pan with butter or oil on medium heat
5. When pan is hot place two fillets at a time until a golden color and crispy
6. Using a flexible non stick spatula turn fish over
7. Repeat with the 2 remaining fish fillets
8. Serve hot
9. Serve with lime wedges, baby tomatoes and favorite greens

Comfort Food!

Ingredients:

4 6-8 ounce skinless cod, sole or catfish fillets
1 Egg, beaten
1/2 Cup fine almond flour
1/2 Cup Coconut flour
1 1/4 Tsp Paprika
1/4 Tsp Cayenne pepper
1 1/2 Tsp Parsley
1 Tsp Pink Himalayan Salt
2 Tsp Dill
1 1/2 Tsp minced dried garlic
Butter, olive oil, or avocado oil for frying

Servings: 4-6

Herbed Mustard Cod With Cauliflower Rice

1. Preheat oven to 375
2. Sprinkle the fish fillets with some salt and pepper and set aside
3. In a blender or Vita Mix combine parsley, garlic, basil, and mustard to create a paste
4. Pour an even amount of herbed paste on each piece of fish
5. Grease an oven proof baking tray with 4 tablespoons of butter, in order for the fish not to stick to the pan when removing and to create a tasty crispy-skinned bottom
6. Bake for 20-25 minutes
7. Serve with a wedge of lime and a side of sauteed cauliflower rice
8. Sprinkle with paprika for color

Ingredients:

4 6 Oz Cod fillets
Sea salt
4 Tbs butter
Ground black pepper
6 Tbs fresh chopped parsley
12 Garlic cloves minced
5 Tsp Mustard (no sugar added dijon preferred)
6 Tbs fresh chopped basil
1 Lime, cut into wedges
Paprika

Servings: 4

Shutterstock / Bartosz Luczak

Tuna Casserole With Mediterranean Sauce

1. Blend sauce ingredients well in a food processor or blender until smooth
2. Preheat oven to 350
3. In a medium size bowl mix together tuna, 4 Tbs butter, cream, salt, garlic powder, cayenne, black pepper, eggs and almond flour until well combined
4. Using the 2 Tbs butter, grease 6 individually portioned size ramekins
5. Pour tuna mixture equally into the 6 greased ramekins and sprinkle with shredded cheese
6. Bake in oven for 30-45 minutes until golden
7. Serve warm with Sauce on the side or drizzled on top

Ingredients:

Casserole:
4 Cans tuna
1/2 Cup heavy cream
4 Eggs
1/2 Cup Almond flour
6 Tbs butter
1 Cup shredded cheese
1 Tsp salt
1/2 Tsp garlic powder
1/4 Tsp black pepper

Mediterranean Sauce:
1 Cup fresh parsley
Juice of 1 lemon
1/2 Tsp salt
1/2 Tsp black pepper
1/4 Tsp cayenne pepper
6 Tbs olive oil

Servings: 6

Baked Avocado, Egg & Smoked Salmon

1. Preheat oven to 375
2. Cut avocados in halves and remove the pits
3. Place the avocados facing up with the peel side on a baking tray
4. Crack each egg into the avocado
5. Fold or roll a slice of smoked salmon beside each egg
6. Sprinkle salt, cayenne and pepper evenly over tops of avocados
7. Bake in oven between 20-25 minutes
8. Serve garnished with freshly chopped parsley and lemon wedges on the side

Ingredients:

4   Avocados cut in halves and pits removed
6   Oz smoked salmon
8   Eggs
1/8 Tsp cayenne pepper
1 Tsp Pink Himalayan Salt
1/2 Tsp black pepper

Garnish:
2   Tbs fresh parsley
2   Lemons cut into 1/4 wedges

Servings: 4

Tuna Croquettes

1. In a bowl mix tuna, almond flour, mayo, eggs, garlic, onion, scallion and salt
2. Form 8 Croquettes
3. Heat oil in pan
4. When oil is ready place patties in pan and fry 2-4 minutes on each side on medium-high heat
5. The patties should be golden
6. Serve with a salad or favorite greens

Ingredients:

24 Oz Solid white canned tuna

3/4 Cup Almond flour

1/4 Cup Primal Kitchen
       Mayonnaise

4 Large eggs

4 Garlic cloves, minced finely

2 Tbs finely grated onion

1 Tsp Pink Himalayan Salt

1 Scallion, cut into thin slices

4 Tbs light olive oil for frying

Servings: 8

Teriyaki Salmon

1. In a bowl stir together all of the Teriyaki sauce ingredients.
2. In a container that can hold 4 slices of salmon pour half the sauce over the fish
3. Put the other half of the sauce in a small container to use for yourself at another time in the refrigerator
4. Place the fish container in the refrigerator for 1-2 hours
5. Preheat indoor grill or broiler
6. Remove fish from sauce & set aside
7. Grill or broil fish for about 3-4 minutes on each side, no longer or it will dry up
8. Transfer the reserved marinade to a small pan
9. Bring to a boil
10. Cook the sauce on medium-low until it is thickened and reduced - about 10 minutes
11. Pour the sauce over the fish
12. Enjoy at room temperature or hot

Helpful Hint:

You'll have leftover marinade from this recipe! It can be kept in the fridge for up to 2 weeks and is delicious on chicken and beef as well as fish.

Ingredients:

1 1/2 Pounds of salmon fillet, cut into 4 slices (each main course serving size is 6 oz)

Teriyaki marinade:
2 1/2 Tbs olive oil
1 1/2 Tbs minced fresh ginger
3 Tbs fresh lemon or lime juice
3 Tbs Wheat-free tamari
3/4 Tsp coarsely ground black pepper
1/4 Tsp cayenne pepper
4 garlic cloves, minced
2 Tbs Lakanto Syrup
4 Scallions, thinly sliced

Servings: 4

Smoked Salmon and Feta Cheese Quiche

1. Preheat oven to 350
2. Whip the eggs
3. Add cut up Smoked Salmon, Feta Cheese, Mozzarella Cheese, salt and pepper and mix well
4. Grease a Quiche Stoneware pan and bake for 30 minutes or until golden

Ingredients:

8 eggs
7 Ounces Smoked Salmon
6 Ounces Mozzarella Cheese
6 Ounces Feta Cheese
1 Tsp Pink Himalayan Salt
Black Pepper to taste

Servings: 4-6

Creamy Lemon Filet Of Fish

1. Preheat Oven to 350
2. Grease pan with butter or oil
3. Place fish filets in oven safe pan
4. Zest 2 lemons over fish
5. Sprinkle salt to taste
6. Sprinkle with ground black pepper
7. Place in oven between 20-25 minutes
8. On the side, heat up a small skillet with cream on medium heat until small bubbles form
9. Reduce heat to medium-low and add the juice of 2 lemons
10. Add the onion powder
11. Reduce heat to low
12. Simmer between 8-10 minutes or until begins to thicken
13. Remove from heat
14. Stir in sour cream
15. Add any remaining juices from the oven-baked fish pan into the creamy sauce
16. When ready for serving, pour creamy sauce over fish
17. Serve with tomato and cucumber on the side seasoned with some olive oil, lemon, parsley flakes, salt & pepper

Ingredients:

6 5-6 oz filet of white fish
such as sole, flounder, cod, halibut, or sea bass
2 Cups heavy cream
1/2 Cup Sour cream
Juice & Zest of 2 Lemons
1 1/2 Tsps onion powder
Ground black pepper to taste
Fine Pink Himalayan Salt

Servings: 6

Shutterstock / Anna Hoychuk

Moroccan Salmon

1. Use a pot a minimum 4-6 inches in depth and 12 inches wide to allow juices to flow freely
2. Cut red pepper in long strips, carrot peeled and cut in thin strips finger size
3. Toss both in pan and sauté with a little olive oil and pink Himalayan salt
4. Add garlic cloves and jalapeños thinly sliced
5. Sauté
6. Add to pan small cubes of tomato
7. Sauté 5 minutes on medium flame
8. Add the olive oil, paprika, black pepper, pink Himalayan salt, and water
9. Let boil for 3 minutes
10. Place lemon slices all around
11. Add Salmon, making sure the fish is halfway covered in liquid
12. Add chopped cilantro sprinkled all over evenly on top of Salmon
13. Cover and let cook 20 minutes on medium heat, then lower for 5 minutes
14. Serve with steamed broccoli and watch people smile

Ingredients:

1 Cup water
1 Large red pepper
4 Garlic cloves peeled
1 Carrot
3 Green jalapeño peppers
1 Small lemon
2 Cups fresh chopped cilantro
1 Large tomato
4 Salmon fillets (4 oz)

Seasonings:
3/4 cup olive oil
2 Flat Tbs paprika
Sprinkle of black pepper
Pink Himalayan salt to taste

Servings: 4-6

Helpful Hint:

When selecting salmon, look at the lines of fat in the salmon. The more lines of fat, the better the salmon will taste. I've never been wrong using this guideline.

Most salmon in supermarkets is farm-raised. The fisheries have to add food color to make it look red to our eyes.

Wild salmon has a different taste but it's much better for you. It is higher in natural omegas.

Most salmon we buy is chinook or king salmon. Coho or silver salmon is also a good choice.

Once a year in June, Copper River Salmon may be available. Your eyes will pop out at the price but it's not to be missed.

Simply the best salmon in the world.

Sublime Salmon

1. Prepare the salmon – Rinse the salmon off and pat it dry. Set aside
2. Now preheat your broiler on high
3. Mix Ingredients
4. Melt butter and mix in all ingredients. You might need to add an additional drop of water
5. Using a brush, apply the chili lime sauce to the salmon which should be in a pan
6. Broil your salmon (on the second shelf) for 10 minutes and look at the salmon
7. Using a fork – check for your level of doneness. It may need another 5 minutes until it's perfect
8. Brush additional sauce on before serving
9. Wash and trim asparagus. Dip in melted butter, sprinkle with Himalayan sea salt and place on pan in the broiler on a middle shelf for 5 minutes, tops. They cook quickly!

Ingredients:

1/2 cup lime juice
(fresh if possible)
2 tbs butter
1 tbs water
1/2 tsp smoky paprika
1/2 tsp za'atar
1.5 tsp chili powder
1 garlic clove, finely minced
1 tbs sweetener
(xylitol, swerve, etc)
1 small onion, diced
4 salmon fillets or steaks

Servings: 4

Instant Salmon in Caramel Sauce

1. Turn your Instant Pot on Saute
2. Add the oil, sweetener, water, tamari, ginger, lime juice, salt and black pepper
3. Simmer the ingredients then turn off
4. Place the fish skin side up (if your fillets come with skin)
5. Spoon the sauce on top of the fish
6. Using your Instant pot on MANUAL, close the pot and seal it
7. Cook on low pressure for 2 minutes
8. Let the pressure release
9. Serve the salmon so the caramelized brown side is face up
10. Garnish with sliced scallions

Ingredients:

1 tablespoon freshly grated ginger
4 6 oz fillets of salmon
1/3 cup Xylitol or Swerve
1 Tsp Pink Himalayan salt
2 Tbsp Wheat Free Tamari
2 Tbsp Water
1/2 Tsp black Pepper
1 Tbsp Lime Juice
1 Tbs olive or coconut oil

Servings: 4

Shutterstock /hlphoto

Blackened Tuna

1. Using a food processor, combine all spices until well blended
2. Transfer to a plate or flat bowl
3. Press each slice of fish into spice mixture on both sides
4. Heat the oil in a frying pan until it is very hot
5. Add the fish to the pan and fry for 2 minutes keeping on high heat
6. Turn fish over and fry for another two minutes - this allows the tuna to remain rare on the inside
7. Serve hot or at room temperature with Salsa on the side or a green vegetable of your choice

Ingredients:

1 1/2 Pounds Skinless and
 Boneless Tuna Fillet
 sliced into 5 pieces
2 Tbs olive oil
1 Tsp Pink Himalayan Salt
1/4 Tsp Ground black pepper
8 Cloves garlic
1 1/2 Tbs paprika
1/2 Tsp Cayenne pepper
1 Tbs Cumin
1 Tbs Oregano
2 Tbs Almond Flour

Servings: 4

Tunisian Spicy Tuna

1. Spray olive oil on a non stick square grill pan set on medium-high heat
2. Sear each side of the tuna steak for a minute or two
3. In a 2 inch deep skillet, Lay onions on the bottom
4. Pour in 1 cup water
5. Pour in tamari, olive oil, fennel powder & crushed garlic
6. Place tomatoes, tuna steaks and peppers evenly
7. Spread jalapeno slices over tuna
8. Drop whole cloves on the sides
9. Turn heat onto medium-high heat covered, preferably using a glass cover to see when it starts to boil
10. When the liquid starts to boil, turn heat to medium-low for 20-25 minutes
11. Remove from skillet carefully, and pour juices over the top
12. Enjoy with the side of slaw

Ingredients:

6 6 oz tuna steaks
1/2 Onion, thinly sliced
6 Jalapenos, sliced
1/4 Cup gluten-free tamari
1/2 Cup olive oil
4 Plum tomatoes, diced
1 1/2 Tbs fennel powder
1 Red pepper, diced
6 Cloves of garlic,
        peeled and crushed
6 Garlic cloves whole with peel

Servings: 6 - 8

Unforgettable Salmon With Garlic and Mustard

This recipe is one of my hidden treasures. It's not on the website and it never will be. It's simple to make but will just blow away your family. They will request it again and again.

1. Preheat the oven to 350 degrees
2. Melt the butter in a saucepan
3. Add the mustard and garlic
4. Stir until mustard is dissolved
5. Using a tablespoon, spoon the mixture on top of the salmon
6. Bake the salmon for 12 minutes; if you like the salmon moist it may be done enough for you. If you like the salmon more well done, rotate the pan in the oven and cook it another 8 minutes or till your desired level of done

Ingredients:

3 tablespoons salted butter
2 tablespoons deli mustard
6-8 cloves of garlic (minced)
6 pieces of salmon fillet

Servings: 6

Cauliflower Rice, Salmon & Avocado Sushi Bomb

1. Using a food processor rice the cauliflower into rice sized pieces by turning on and off quickly (check your local supermarket to see the availability of Cauliflower Rice in the freezer section)
2. In a high heated pan cook cauliflower rice with the Wheat-free tamari stirring quickly until most of the liquid is dried out
3. Transfer cauliflower to a bowl and combine with cream cheese & apple cider vinegar
4. Place in refrigerator to cool for 30 minutes
5. Put a nori sheet down on a bamboo roller sheet which should be covered with plastic wrap to prevent sticking
6. Spread a very thin layer of cauliflower rice evenly over the entire nori sheet leaving a little less than an inch of space along the top of nori sheet
7. Place salmon bits, cucumber strips, scallion and avocado in an even line across starting at about 1 inch from the bottom of the nori sheet
8. Start to roll sushi tightly using bamboo roller sheet, starting at the bottom end
9. Serve and enjoy with pickled ginger, wasabi or a spicy mayo you can make yourself using:
   1/4 Cup Primal Kitchen Mayo
   1/4 Tsp cayenne pepper
   1 Tsp freshly squeezed lime juice

Ingredients:

6 Ounces fresh raw salmon, chopped
7 Ounces cream cheese
5 Sheets of Nori Seaweed sheets
2 Tbs Apple cider vinegar
1 1/2 Tbs Wheat-free tamari
1 Large cucumber, sliced in 3 inch long, thin strips
1 Avocado, sliced thin
3 Scallions, chopped very small
2 Cups cauliflower

Servings: 4 - 6

Spicy Tuna Sushi Bomb

1. Using a food processor, chop the cauliflower into rice-sized pieces by turning on and off quickly
2. Sauté cauliflower rice in a pan with oil, Swerve, vinegar, and salt for 5-10 minutes until water is absorbed
3. Place in refrigerator to cool for 30 minutes
4. Put a nori sheet down on a bamboo roller sheet which should be covered with plastic wrap to prevent sticking
5. Spread a very thin layer of cauliflower rice evenly over the entire nori sheet leaving a little less than an inch of space along the top of nori sheet
6. Place Spicy tuna mixture in a row across
7. Put a few pieces of avocado and cucumber strips on top of the tuna mix
8. Start to roll sushi tightly using bamboo roller sheet, starting at the bottom end
9. Serve with a small dipping bowl of spicy mayo

Ingredients:

Spicy Tuna Mix:
5 Ounces Sushi-grade tuna, chopped
3 Scallions, chopped very thin
1/8 Tsp black pepper
1/2 Tsp cayenne pepper
1 Tsp Wheat-free tamari
1/2 Tsp coconut oil
1/2 Avocado sliced thin
1 Small cucumber sliced into very thin strips

Cauliflower Rice:
10 Ounces Cauliflower rice
1/2 Tsp coconut oil
1/2 Tsp Swerve Sweetener
1/2 Tsp Apple cider vinegar
1/8 Tsp Pink Himalayan salt

Spicy Mayo Dip:
1/4 Cup Primal Kitchen Mayo
1/4 Tsp Cayenne pepper
1 Tsp freshly squeezed lime juice

Servings: 4

Fathead Pizza (& Nicoise)

Fathead pizza is a very popular recipe floating around Keto sites. This recipe adds spices to the crust, suggests you oil the parchment paper, and roll the dough out thin. Because every oven is different, make sure to check your oven often so it doesn't burn.

1. Mix the shredded/grated cheese and almond flour/meal in a microwaveable bowl. Add the cream cheese and stir
2. Microwave on high for 1 minute. Stir again. Then microwave on high for another 30 seconds
3. Add the egg, salt, basil , garlic and any other flavorings you choose and mix gently
4. Place between 2 greased pieces of baking parchment/paper and roll into a circular pizza shape
5. Remove the top baking paper/parchment. If the mixture hardens and becomes difficult to work with, pop it back in the microwave for 10-20 seconds to soften again - but not too long or you will cook the egg
6. Make fork holes all over the pizza base to ensure it cooks evenly
7. Slide the baking paper/parchment with the pizza base, on a baking sheet or pizza stone
8. Bake at 425F for 12 minutes or until brown. Don't burn it!
9. Once cooked, remove from the oven, spread the tomato sauce evenly as close to the edges as possible to prevent burning, and add all of the toppings. Put it back in the oven for 5-10 minutes.

Ingredients:

Dough:
1 3/4 cups shredded
    mozzarella cheese
3/4 cup almond meal/flour
2 tbsp cream cheese
1 egg
pinch Himalayan salt to taste
½ tsp dried basil
½ tsp garlic powder

Toppings:
Shredded Cheese – Cheddar
    and/or Mozzarella
Sliced tomato
Onion, diced
Fresh garlic

for Nicoise:
1 Can solid white tuna
Green, black or kalamata olives
    cut in half

Garnish:
Crushed red pepper or
whatever spice you enjoy !

Servings: 8

Pepper Steak & Salad

1. Marinate steaks for about 30 minutes in steak seasoning
2. Slice red peppers and red onion
3. Cook Steaks in either a large skillet to reserve the flavorful juices or broil in your oven on each side a few minutes until done
4. When steaks are almost ready, place sliced up pepper and onion under the broiler or on the side of the steak in the skillet and toss until cooked
5. You can do this by cooking 2 steaks at a time with the veggies in your skillet or broiler pan, if you don't have room for all 4 steaks at the same time along with the veggies
6. This process gives the red pepper and onion a lot of flavor
7. Set Aside after ready
8. In a bowl mix the spinach, lettuce or spring greens, cucumbers & tomatoes cut into 1/8 wedges
9. Add the hearts of palm cut up on top
10. Pour dressing over and toss lightly
11. Plate each steak with the pepper, onion & reserved juices over the steak, served with the salad

Ingredients:

Steak:
4   Steaks up to 6 oz
2 Tsp Ground Black Pepper
3 Tsp Garlic Powder
3 Tbs Olive Oil
2 Tbs Wheat-free tamari

Salad:
7 oz Baby spinach greens
7 oz spring greens
2 Vine ripened tomatoes
1 Cucumber
3 Red peppers
1 Red onion
1 Can of hearts of palm

Dressing:
2 Tbs lemon juice
1 Tsp black pepper
1/4 Cup olive oil
1 Tsp sea salt

Servings: 4

Beef Fajitas & Bell Peppers

1. Heat fajita skillet with olive oil until hot
2. Place meat in skillet
3. Toss every 1 minute or so
4. Cook until beef looks cooked through
5. Add vegetables
6. Stir-fry until tender
7. Serve over cooked cauliflower rice

Ingredients:

1½ lb round bottom steaks
sliced into strip slices
1 Small red onion, diced
3 Tbs Mild olive oil
2 Tsp Sea Salt
2 Tsp garlic powder
2 Tsp onion powder
3/4 Tsp ginger powder
3/4 Tsp celery seed
1 Tsp ground coriander
1 Tsp Cumin
1 Red bell pepper, sliced
   into thin strips
1 Green bell pepper, sliced
   into thin strips

Servings: 4 -6

Stuffed Peppers

1. Preheat oven to 350
2. Remove tops of peppers including the seeds and chop up what you removed for later
3. Place peppers upright in a greased baking dish
4. Heat 2 tablespoons of oil in a skillet over medium-high heat
5. Add beef, season with salt and pepper and cook by allowing to brown nicely
6. Transfer to a plate
7. Pour 2 tablespoons of oil in heated skillet, add the onions and chopped bits of the top of the pepper and saute well
8. Add the garlic, zucchini, tomatoes, cayenne or chili pepper, salt & black pepper
9. Cook until well done and then add cooked cauliflower rice and beef
10. Taste to adjust salt, pepper and perhaps the heat from the cayenne or chili pepper before filling peppers
11. Fill peppers
12. Pour a small amount of water into the bottom of the baking dish and drizzle remaining oil over the filled peppers
13. Cover and bake for 25 minutes
14. Uncover and bake another 25 minutes or until top is golden

Ingredients:

6 Red bell peppers
6 Tbs light olive oil
10 Ounces ground beef
Kosher salt
Ground black pepper
1 large onion, diced
4 Garlic cloves minced
1 Zucchini, diced
4 Small tomatoes, seeded and finely diced
2 Tsp Cayenne or chili powder
1 Cup cooked cauliflower rice

Servings: 6

Shutterstock / Elena Shashkina

Shepherd's Pie

1. Using a large stove top pan heat up oil on medium heat
2. Chop one onion in small pieces and toss in pan to sizzle and brown
3. When onions are browning add diced red pepper.
4. Add ground beef and stir until done. Stir often because the meat cooks quickly.
5. Use coconut oil to grease lasagna pan.
6. Pour meat in the the bottom of the pan and let cool.
7. Add riced cauliflower and remaining onion and eggs to food processor.
8. Add salt and pepper
9. Process until creamy texture
10. Pour over browned meat in lasagna pan
11. Bake in oven at 350 for 30 minutes
12. Take out of oven briefly and put some coconut oil on the top to help brown the mixture
13. Put back in oven for another 30 minutes
14. Garnish with parsley

Ingredients:

2 Large onions
2 lbs ground beef
6 eggs
3 Packages Riced Cauliflower
1 1/2 Tsp Pink Himalayan salt
1/2 Tsp Pepper
1 finally diced red pepper
2 Tbs olive or coconut oil
Sprig of parsley to garnish

Servings: 6-8

Moist Vegetable Meat Loaf

1. Preheat oven to 350
2. Using a large mixing bowl, place meat inside and set aside
3. Using a food processor on a pulse setting chop all vegetables, including garlic cloves until very small. This step may need to be repeated more than one time, allowing space for all of the vegetables to be properly chopped finely
4. Transfer ground up vegetables to the bowl with meat and add almond flour, salt, pepper and eggs and mix very well
5. Separate meat into two parts on a work surface, and create two separate rolls which resemble small log like shapes pressing meat mixture together tightly
6. Grease two loaf pans well
7. Place rolls of meat into loaf pans
8. Bake 1 hour
9. Remove from oven and allow to stand a few minutes before slicing

Ingredients:

2 Pounds grounds beef
1 Zuchini, peeled and chopped
1 Large vidalia onion, quartered
1 Carrot, peeled and cut
7 Oz portabella mushrooms, chopped
1/4 Head of broccoli, chopped
1/4 Head of cauliflower, chopped
4 stalks celery, chopped
5 cloves of garlic
1/2 Cup Almond flour
1 1/2 tsp kosher salt
1 Tsp black pepper
5 eggs, beaten well

Servings: 10

Shutterstock / Timolina

Beef Kebabs

1. Slice an onion and red pepper separately on the side
2. Mix all ingredients together using your hands to combine well
3. Using skewers with a handful of ground beef wrap meat by applying some pressure around skewers, not too thick, so the meat will cook through and not fall off the skewers during the grilling process
4. Place Kebabs on grill on medium heat
5. When meat is partially cooked, grill sliced onion and red pepper on the side
6. Leave Kebabs and vegetables on grill on medium heat until golden
7. Plate Kebabs and grilled veggies
8. Serve with a small bowl of Tehini on the side

Ingredients:

3 Pounds ground beef
2 Medium onions chopped into very small cubes
1 Cup finely chopped parsley
1 Tsp black black pepper
1 Tsp kosher salt
1 1/2 Tsp paprika
2 Tbs light olive oil

Servings: 6 - 8

Homemade Barbecue Ribs

1. Prepare the Completely Keto Memphis Barbecue Sauce (recipe on page 155)
2. Rub each rib very well and place inside air fryer and follow cooking instructions if using for the first time
3. Cook for 20-30 minutes until gold in color

Ingredients:

2 short ribs per person as appetizer or 4 pieces per person as a main course

Holiday Roast

1. Preheat oven to 350 degrees
2. Combine all ingredients for the sauce in a food processor until smooth
3. Place the brisket in a pan that just fits the meat so that the meat is sitting in the sauce
4. Pour the sauce over the meat
5. Cover tightly with two layers of aluminum foil
6. Bake for two hours or less depending on how you like your meat, use the thermometer to check after one hour
7. Take cover off and turn meat over and bake uncovered for 1 hour or check with a thermometer inserted in its center to cook according to how you, your family and your guests prefer. For more medium cooked roasts, check with a thermometer after 1 hour of baking and after two hours and so on
8. Transfer meat to a cutting board and allow to cool for 10 minutes. If you cut the meat too quickly, it tends to shred.
9. Pour sauce from the pan into a stovetop saucepan and cook on medium-high heat until it is reduced to under 3 cups
10. Slice meat against the grain
11. Pour the sauce on top and serve hot

Ingredients:

Sauce:
1 Onion cut in 4
1 3" piece of fresh ginger, peeled
10 Garlic cloves
1/4 Cup Deli Mustard
1/2 Cup Pinot Noir
1/2 Cup Zevia Cola or Ginger Ale
1 Cup Homemade Ketchup (pg. 156)
1/2 Lakanto Sweetener
1/4 Cup apple cider vinegar
1/4 Cup Wheat-free tamari
1/2 Cup olive oil
1/2 Tsp ground cloves
1 Tbs Coarse Ground black pepper

1 first-cut brisket, 6-7 pounds, rinsed and patted dry

Servings: 12

Spaghetti And Meatballs

1. Prepare Miracle Noodles according to package directions and set aside
2. In a skillet heat up oil and sauté onions, mushrooms, celery and peppers until soft on low-medium heat
3. Add salt, pepper, cayenne, paprika, garlic and Swerve granular sweetener and put on low heat
4. Add tomato paste and juice and cover
5. In a separate pan brown 1/4 pound meat and add to sauce
6. Cover and keep on low heat
7. In a large bowl mix meatball ingredients and form into small balls and carefully drop into sauce
8. Keep on low heat for one hour covered
9. Serve over miracle noodles

Ingredients:

Miracle Noodles

Meatballs:
1 1/4 Pounds ground beef
1 Egg
1/4 Cup Almond flour
1/4 Cup water
2 Tbs Homemade Ketchup
    (pg. 156)
1/8 Tsp salt
1/4 Tsp black pepper

Sauce:
1 20-Ounce can of tomato juice
1 6-Ounce can of tomato paste
1 Tsp Swerve granular
2 Garlic cloves minced finely
1 1/4 Tsp paprika
1/4 Tsp Cayenne pepper
1/2 Tsp Pink Himalayan Salt
1/2 Tsp Black pepper
2 Green peppers, cut into cubes
4 Stalks celery, cut into cubes
1 Large onion, chopped3/4
Pound Portabella mushrooms,
    cut into small pieces
2 Tbs Coconut oil

Servings: 6

Meatballs With Artichoke Hearts

1. Add meat, chopped parsley, and half an onion to a bowl.
2. Sprinkle salt to taste
3. Set aside
4. Using a medium size pot, heat pot for one minute then add a little coconut oil
5. Add the rest of your onions on a medium flame
6. Meanwhile onion starts to caramelize (slightly cooked)
7. Cut tomato into small tiny cubes and then add them to the pot once onions look slightly cooked.
8. Sauté together for 2 minutes
9. Add your seasonings
10. Mix for a few seconds
11. Then add 1 cup of water letting it come to a boil leaving on medium flame
12. Get your bowl of meat
13. Start making round small meat balls by adding them to the sauce
14. Add your artichoke hearts cut in half
15. Cover let cook for 30 minutes on medium low flame

Ingredients:

1 pound ground meat
1 cup chopped parsley
2 large onions, chopped
1 tomato
1 package frozen artichoke hearts
4 tbs olive oil
2 tsp cumin
1 tsp paprika
1 tsp Himalayan salt

Servings: 4

Corned Beef

Curing the Meat
1. Find a large pot and put the meat in it
2. Add the distilled water, kosher salt, pink salt, and pickling spice and the cloves together. Stir well.
3. Add the brisket to the curing solution and put in the refrigerator
4. Add the meat to the curing solution. If it floats put a plastic container filled with brine on top of it to force it down. Make sure to completely cover the meat with the brine. Leave it cure in the pot for 7 days. Stir the solution once a day
5. When the meat is done it may be red, tan or even gray

Cooking the Meat
1. Dump out the brine.
2. Simmer it in a pot. Simmer for a half hour, dump out the water. Add fresh water and cook on low heat for 3 hours
3. Let cool before slicing

Ingredients:

About 4 pounds of beef brisket
1 gallon distilled water
8 ounces kosher salt
    (about 7/8 of a cup)
2 teaspoons pink curing salt
    (Note: This is not
    Himalayan Salt)
6 tablespoons pickling spice
4 pressed or cut up cloves of garlic

Servings: 8 - 10

Shutterstock / Janet Moore

"I Want More" Keto Meatloaf

Curing the Meat

1. Mix together ingredients for the topping and set aside
2. Preheat oven to 350
3. Melt coconut oil or olive oil in skillet or pan. Sauté onion
4. Soak almond flour in almond milk
5. Combine all ingredients and mix well
6. Pour into 10x5 loaf pan
7. Spread topping on top of loaf
8. Bake from 45 minutes to one hour

Helpful Hint:

Make sure to choose a meat with a good fat content.
If you use a lean ground beef, it will come out dry.

Ingredients:

Topping:
1/2 cup Homemade Ketchup
        (pg 156) or BBQ Sauce
        (pg 155)
2 tbs Lakanto sweetener
2 tbs apple cider vinegar

Meatloaf:
2 tbs of coconut oil
        or extra virgin olive oil
1 small onion, finely chopped
2 cups of extra fine almond flour
1/4 cup unsweetened almond milk
2 pounds of ground beef
2 eggs
2 tbs of ground white horseradish
        (no sugar no soy)
2 tbs kosher salt
1/4 tsp freshly ground
        black pepper
1 tsp dry mustard
1/4 cup Homemade Ketchup
        (pg 156) or BBQ Sauce
        (pg 155)

Servings: 8

Sweet & Sour Hot Dogs

1. Cut up the hot dogs into small 1 inch pieces
2. Place in pot and add mustard and Lakanto syrup
3. Cook on low heat for an hour
4. Stir occasionally with a wooden spoon
5. Serve over riced cauliflower
6. Pour the extra sauce on the cauliflower

Ingredients:

2 packages of hot dogs.
1 16 oz jar of deli mustard
1 cup of Lakanto syrup

Servings: 8

Helpful Hint:

Only use all beef hot dogs with no nitrates and no preservatives.
Be sure to read the ingredients for hidden sugars, cereals, and carbs.

Silvertip Roast

1. Place onion on the bottom of a roasting pan.
2. Top with meat (rinse off with water first)
3. Preheat the oven to 375
4. Combine garlic, oil, and all spices in a bowl and cover the meat.
5. Let it sit for an hour or two to absorb the flavors
6. Combine the wine, water, and ketchup and pour over the meat.
7. Insert an oven thermometer into the thickest part of the meat.
8. Place in the oven uncovered for 45 minutes
9. Cover the meat and let it cook until the thermometer shows 135 degrees
10. The meat will be rare at that time BUT… the meat continues to cook after you take it out of the oven.
11. Let the meat cool for 30-45 minutes before slicing thin.
12. Cover with juices and warm it up in the oven if you like well done

Ingredients:

Large onion, sliced
5 lbs silvertip Roast beef
5 cloves garlic, crushed
1 Tsp Pink Himalayan salt
1/2 Tsp Black Pepper
1 Tsp Sweet Paprika
3 Tbs olive or coconut oil
1 Tsp cumin
1/2 cup Pinot Noir
1/2 cup water (or 1 cup if you don't
    use the wine above)
1 cup of Homemade Ketchup
    (pg 156)

Servings: 16 - 18

Prime Rib of Beef With Wine and Garlic

1. Preheat your oven to 450 degrees
2. Using a very sharp knife, cut slits in the meat and put a clove of garlic in each slit
3. Place salt and pepper on the meat. Be generous
4. Put the onions in the bottom of a roasting pan
5. Place the meat on top of the onions
6. After 30 minutes, lower the oven temperature to 300
7. Use a digital thermometer to check the temperature after 30 minutes
8. Take the meat out at 130 degrees for medium rare, 140 degrees for medium. The meat will continue to cook slightly after it's out of the over so don't overcook the meat
9. Take the beef broth and wine and combine them in a saucepan. Add the juice from the pan. Bring to a boil
10. When you are ready to carve the meat, cut generous portions in between the bones. This serves 12-14 hungry eaters.

Ingredients:

1 12-14 lb bone in prime rib
        beef roast with 6 ribs
8 whole cloves of garlic
        with peel removed.
2 medium yellow onions,
        peeled and quartered
¾ cup Pinot Noir or Cabernet
2 cups of beef broth
salt
freshly ground black pepper

Servings: 12 - 14

Shutterstock / Istetiana

Stuffed Cabbage

1. Remove and save the core from the cabbage
2. Steam the cabbage until it softens
3. Allow it to Cool
4. Peel off the leaves. Save any broken leaves.
5. Combine the meat, eggs, cauliflower rice, almond flour, and Himalayan salt and mix well
6. In the bottom of a large pot brown your onion in coconut oil
7. Add your tomatoes and all the pieces of cabbage that didn't make the grade (the broken pieces), the lemon juice, and the Lakanto
8. Using whole leaves of cabbage add some of the meat mixture and make rolls
9. Gently add the stuffed cabbage rolls to the pot
10. Cook on a low heat for 2 hours
11. In a flat pan, arrange the cabbage
12. Pour in the juice
13. Sprinkle the top with Lakanto golden sweetener
14. Bake at 325 for one hour

Ingredients:

1 Whole Cabbage
4 lbs of chopped meat
3 Whole eggs
1 lb Package of cauliflower rice
1/4 cup Almond flour
1 tsp Himalayan salt
1 large onion, chopped
4 fresh tomatoes, chopped or
       1 can of tomatoes
1/4 cup Lemon juice
1/2 cup liquid Lakanto
       sweetener

Servings: 10 - 12

Beef and Broccoli

1. In a wok or frying pan add two tablespoons of olive oil.
2. Cook over a medium heat. This cooks fast!
3. Add onion, ginger, and garlic to the pan.
4. Add sliced beef. (Some times they have it labeled pepper steak but any thin cut beef works)
5. Let brown for a few moments and stir
6. Add broccoli florets to the mixture.
7. Add 1/4 cup Wheat-free tamari to the mix.
8. Cook the broccoli to taste. Some might want to add an optional teaspoon of swerve to the mix
9. Serve over riced cauliflower.
10. Pour the extra sauce on the cauliflower

Ingredients:

1 Small onion, chopped
1 small piece of ginger, minced
1 clove of garlic, minced
1 pound of sliced beef
4 cups of broccoli florets
1/4 cup Wheat-free tamari
1 tsp Swerve (optional)

Servings: 4 - 6

Helpful Hint:

This dinner cooks up quickly! Don't blink or walk away from the pan.

Shutterstock / Ruslan Mitin

Perfect Brisket

1. 24 hours in advance, take out the meat and rinse it off. Rub olive oil all over the meat
2. Then cover the meat with Completely Keto BBQ Rub and leave it in the refrigerator for 24 hours
3. Make sure to get both sides of the meat
4. Turn on your grill. If, like most folks, you have a 3 burner gas grill, turn on only the front burner and let the grill warm up
5. If you can cook with wood chips, add them before you turn on the grill
6. Place the meat the grill AWAY from the flame
7. Now close the grill and go away for 1 hour. No peeking. After an hour flip the meat over
8. After 2 hours, put the meat in an aluminum pan. Cover the pan so the meat doesn't dry out or double wrap the meat in aluminum foil. (Double wrap to prevent ripping)
9. Leave the meat on the grill a total of six hours
10. Take the meat off the grill and upwrap. Coat the meat with my BBQ sauce
11. Wrap the meat up again and let it sit for one hour
12. Thinly slice the meat

Ingredients:

1 Brisket
Completely Keto BBQ Rub
(pg 154)

Servings: 8

Overnight Brisket

1. Rinse off the meat.
2. Assemble all ingredients in an aluminum pan
3. Add water in the pan until it's 3/4 up the side of the meat.
4. Turn the oven on to 250 degrees and GO TO SLEEP
5. When you wake up, the house will smell delicious and your brisket will be done
6. It should cook for a minimum of six hours
7. Let the meat sit for one hour
8. Thinly slice the meat

Helpful Hint:

Many years ago I spoke with the owner of Corky's BBQ. It's the largest BBQ place in Memphis. He told me the real secret to great 'Q is the meat. Make sure to choose an inexpensive cut of meat.

For brisket, do NOT chose a first cut or top of the rib. I buy second cut brisket. If all they have are lean cuts of meat, talk to the butcher.

You want a fatty cut of meat.

Ingredients:

1 Brisket
8 minced cloves of garlic
2 medium onion, chopped
1/4 cup extra virgin olive oil, divided
1 bunch of celery, peeled and sliced
1 large can tomatoes, diced or crushed
1/2 cup Lakanto sweetener
1/4 apple cider vinegar
Salt and pepper

Servings: 8

Rack of Lamb

1. In a small bowl mix olive oil, garlic, lemon juice, fresh rosemary, red pepper flakes and salt
2. Using an oven safe porcelain dish, place the rack of lamb side by side with the tips facing up
3. Pour spice mixture over the rack of lamb
4. Cover and place in the refrigerator for about 6-8 hours
5. Preheat oven to 375
6. Remove lamb from the refrigerator and allow to rest for an hour or so
7. Roast in oven for 20 minutes
8. Lower oven temperature to 325 and continue roasting for 45-55 minutes or until lamb looks ready and golden in color
9. Remove from oven, slice and drizzle juices over when serving

Ingredients:

2 Racks of lamb,
    about 6 bones each
1 Tsp dry red pepper flakes
3/4 Cup olive oil
Juice of 1 small lemon
8 Large garlic cloves,
    finely minced
2 Tbs chopped fresh rosemary
1 1/2 Tsp coarse Pink
    Himalayan Salt

Servings: 6

Tomato Pesto Pie

1. Use a rectangular pie tray at least 12 x 15 or larger
2. Mix the shredded/grated cheese and almond flour/meal in a microwaveable bowl. Add the cream cheese and stir
3. Microwave on HIGH for 1 minute. Stir again. Then microwave on HIGH for another 30 seconds
4. Add the egg, salt, basil , garlic, pepper and any other flavorings you choose and mix gently
5. Place pie crust in between 2 (butter/oil) greased pieces of baking parchment/paper and place onto a rectangular shape large pie tray
6. Remove only top parchment paper after dough is in baking pan reaching all corners and edges and thickness is spread evenly, using your fingers to feel the doughs thickness on top of the paper
7. Keep the bottom parchment paper under pie crust while baking
8. Make fork holes all over the dough to ensure it cooks evenly
9. Bake at 425F for exactly 12 minutes or until golden
10. Remove from oven and allow to cool
11. Spread Pesto Sauce all over pie crust
12. Slice tomatoes and place all around in whichever way you choose
13. Sprinkle salt & pepper over the tomatoes and bake in oven between 5-10 minutes, depending how well done you like the tomatoes
14. Please watch carefully as every oven varies in temperature
15. Slice into small squares

Ingredients:

Crust:
1 3/4 cups pre shredded/
        grated cheese
3/4 cup almond meal/flour
2 tbsp cream cheese
1 egg
Himalayan salt to taste
½ tsp of dried basil and
        garlic powder

Pesto Sauce:
1 Cup fresh basil leaves
1/4 Cup Pili nuts
1/3 Cup olive oil
2 Tbs Primal Kitchen Mayo
3 Cloves fresh garlic

4-6 Tomatoes, sliced thin
Fresh ground pepper
Salt

Servings: 12

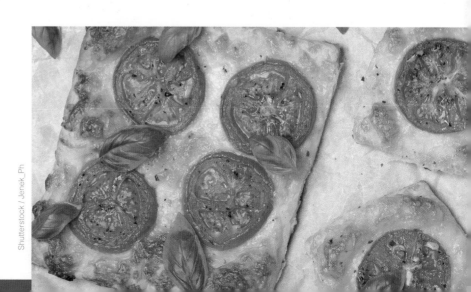

Shutterstock / Jenek_Ph

Skillet Salami & Grilled Onion Sunny Side Up Eggs

1. Using an indoor grill or heavy skillet grill onion chopped into fine slivered slices in 2 tbs coconut oil or butter
2. Add salami slices around skillet and brown on each side on top of the onions
3. Add eggs cracked over salami and sprinkle salt, pepper and oregeno all over the top
4. Cover and cook on low for 3-5 minutes depending if you prefer the eggs runny or cooked through
5. Serve with mustard on the side
6. Garnish with greens

Ingredients:

8 Oz Salami sliced thin
2 Extra large eggs
1 Large Vidalia onion
2 Tbs coconut oil or butter
1 Tsp Pink Himalayan Salt
1/2 Tsp ground black pepper
1 Tsp ground Oregeno

Servings: 2

Keto Mushroom And Tomato Omelet

1. Using a large stove top pan heat up oil on medium heat
2. Chop onion in small squares and toss in pan to sizzle and brown
3. Whisk eggs and pour in pan over onions
4. Slice mushrooms in thin slices and place evenly over eggs
5. Use 1 Tsp water and mix salt and pepper together and pour over mushrooms and eggs
6. Slice Tomato thinly and place gently over eggs in a decorative manner
7. Sprinkle Mozzarella cheese over empty areas
8. Change temperature to low-medium heat
9. Cover and cook until eggs are not runny
10. Garnish with Parsley chopped finely on top
11. Remove from heat and slide onto a platter and serve in triangle portions

Ingredients:

1 Large onion
10 eggs
1 Package mushrooms
    (of your choice)
      6 ounces or more
1 Tsp Pink Himalayan salt
1/2 Tsp Pepper
1 Large or two medium
    tomatoes
1 Tbs olive oil
4 Ounces Mozzarella cheese,
    shredded
Sprig of parsley to garnish

Servings: 4 - 6

Pizza Omelette

Okay you're laughing at me. Harlan why are you wasting your time teaching us how to make an omelette?

My answer is that not everyone knows how to cook an omelette. Besides, this is my recipe and it may be different than yours. Enjoy.

1. Lightly Mix together onion, garlic, black pepper, and eggs.
2. Heat Up Pan
3. Add 2 tablespoons of coconut oil or Kerry Gold Grass fed butter to pan
4. Allow to melt
5. Add egg mixture and turn up heat until it starts to cook
6. Add tomato sauce
7. Add mozzarella cheese
8. Fold the omelette into half
9. Cook both sides

Ingredients:

1 Onion, medium, finely chopped
2 Garlic cloves, minced
1/2 tsp ground Black pepper
3 whole eggs
4 Tbs of sugar free
 tomato sauce
1/4 cup mozzarella cheese

Servings: 1

Vegetable Quiche Lorraine

1. Preheat Oven to 350
2. Using a large Saute skillet put enough coconut oil to cover the bottom of the pan
3. Put all ingredients except for the eggs and coconut milk into the pan and saute for about 10 minutes stirring every minute or so
4. Grease a large round quiche pan with coconut oil
5. Pour vegetable mixture into the quiche pan
6. Gently pour egg and coconut milk mixture over the vegetables
7. Bake in oven for 25 minutes and eggs are not runny on top

Ingredients:

6 ounces of cauliflower florets in small pieces
6 ounces of broccoli florets in small pieces
2 Zuchini, cut in thin circles and in half
5 Oz whole cherry tomatoes
1 Yellow bell pepper, diced
1 Red bell pepper, diced
5 Oz portabella mushrooms, chopped
2 ounces fresh basil, chopped
1 Tsp Pink Himalayan Salt
4 Garlic cloves minced
1/2 Tsp black pepper
10 Eggs with 1/2 cup coconut milk, beaten together

Servings: 4

Pancakes With Fresh Blueberries

This pancake recipe calls for 4 servings by making either 1 regular pancake or a few small appetizer size pancakes which is easier to make in the pan when pouring the batter.

1. Mash blueberries in a small bowl using a spatula
2. In a separate small bowl beat the egg whites until peaks begin to form and set aside
3. In a medium sized bowl mix all other ingredients with the egg yolks
4. Combine blueberries, egg whites and pancake mixture & mix together by folding gently
5. Heat skillet with butter
6. Pour in batter according to the size pancake you would like
7. Allow to cook on the first side until it looks golden on the bottom and then flip over and do the same
8. Serve with Lakanto syrup and a handful of fresh blueberries on top

Ingredients:

4 Large eggs
1/4 Cup Blueberries
4 Tsp Swerve Granular
6 Oz blanched almond flour
4 Oz heavy whipping cream
1/8 Tsp Fine Pink Himalayan Salt
1/4 Tsp Vanilla extract
1/2 Tsp baking powder
2 Tbs butter for the pan

Servings: 4

Spanish Omelette

1. Melt butter in a heated skillet
2. Saute celery slices in skillet
3. Add all seasonings
4. Toss for 3-5 minutes on medium-low heat or until desired tenderness is reached
5. Add Spinach and mix well
6. Beat eggs
7. Move vegetable mix to the side of the skillet
8. Pour beaten eggs on the other side of the skillet
9. Gently fold vegetable mix onto eggs
10. Cook covered or uncovered for 2-3 minutes

Ingredients:

6 Eggs
2 Tbs butter
4 Stalks of celery chopped into small slices
6 Oz baby spinach
2 Tsp tumeric
1 Tsp cumin
1/2 Tsp Pink Himalayan Salt
1/4 Tsp black pepper

Servings: 2

Eggplant Parmesan

1. Preheat oven to 375
2. On a piece of parchment paper and butter, line Eggplant slices out evenly and sprinkle with salt
3. Bake for 20 minutes
4. Remove from oven
5. Grease a porcelain 9 x 13 inch baking tray with butter
6. Place half the eggplant slices at the bottom
7. Top with half of the marinara sauce and set aside
8. In a pot, cook the cauliflower for 5 minutes on low in water
9. Remove cauliflower and keep 1/4 cup of the liquid
10. In a blender make a paste of the frozen cauliflower, 1/4 cup of the cooking water, greek yogurt and salt
11. After the layer of marinara sauce, spread half of the cauliflower paste evenly over and sprinkle half of the mozzarella cheese around, then repeat with placing the eggplant slices and marinara and cauliflower paste again ending with sprinkling the remaining cheese over at the end
12. Bake for 30-40 minutes until golden

Ingredients:

1 Large eggplant
2 Cups No Sugar Added
     Marinara sauce
6 Ounces shredded
     mozzarella cheese
1 12 Oz Bag riced cauliflower
1/4 Cup water from
     cooking cauliflower
1 Full fat 3 Oz container of
     plain Greek yogurt
1 Tsp sea salt

Servings: 6

Falafel Balls

1. In a large bowl mix all ingredients except for the oil
2. In a small skillet heat up oil about 1/2 inch high
3. Use an ice cream scooper to make 10 balls
4. Fry a few at a time for about 3-4 minutes on each side until begins to brown
5. Remove and serve with the Tehini Sauce recipe found in this book

Ingredients:

1 Tsp Pink Himalayan Salt
3 Garlic cloves minced
1 Cup riced cauliflower
3/4 Cup Almond flour
1 Tbs cumin
1 Tsp cayenne pepper
4 Tbs Parsley, chopped finely
2 Large eggs
Light olive oil for cooking

Servings: 5

Four Cheese Zucchini And Cauliflower Gratin

1. Preheat oven to 350
2. Melt butter in a small saucepan, add in Xanthan gum and cream and combine well
3. Bring to a boil over medium-high heat and cook for two minutes
4. Season sauce with 1 teaspoon salt, 1 teaspoon black pepper and 2 cloves of minced garlic, and set aside
5. Place thawed cauliflower in a colander and press down to get most of the liquid out
6. In a large bowl, toss cauliflower with the sauce and cut up in small bits, 1 oz of each cheese inside and mix well and set aside
7. In a separate bowl, cut up the 4 types of cheeses with 2 teaspoons salt, 1 teaspoon black pepper and 4 minced garlic cloves and toss well
8. Grease bottom of casserole dish with the remaining 2 tablespoons of butter
9. Line bottom of dish with 1 layer of zucchini slices
10. Sprinkle 4 cheese mixture on top of zucchini layer evenly
11. Repeat, and place the zucchini slices in an even layer on top of cheeses and again add a layer of cheese until you have no more left
12. Take cauliflower bowl, and stir around a couple of times before pouring cauliflower mixture on top of the zuchini and cheese layers
13. After pouring cauliflower mixture in, take a spoon and even out the layer of cauliflower on top
14. Bake in oven for 50-60 minutes
15. Optional: garnish with chopped scallions

Ingredients:

2 12 Oz Bags of frozen cauliflower florets, thawed & drained
8 Zucchini, Sliced thin
4 Tbs butter
1 1/2 Cups heavy whipping cream
3 Tsp Pink Himalayan Salt
1 Tsp Xanthan Gum
6 Oz mozzarella cheese
6 Oz provolone cheese
6 Oz cheddar cheese
6 Oz colby cheese
6 Garlic cloves, minced finely
2 Tsp black pepper

Servings: 8

Zoodles and Homemade Tomato Basil Sauce

1. Wash and dry zuchini
2. Using a Zoodle Maker, create any size zoodle you prefer and set aside
3. In a medium size saucepan, saute onions for 5 minutes in olive oil on medium-high
4. Reduce heat to medium-low
5. Add minced garlic and stir 2 minutes
6. Toss in diced tomatoes and cook 5 more minutes
7. Pour tomato paste, water, and swerve into the pan and stir while cooking 2 more minutes
8. Add basil, paprika, pepper and salt and cook for 10 minutes, covered
9. Keep warm until ready to serve
10. Heat up the Zoodles for 45 seconds in a microwave safe plate
11. Serve the sauce warm over Zoodles and enjoy!

Ingredients:

8 Zuchini

Tomato Sauce:
1 Large onion, chopped
6 Cloves minced garlic
1/4 Tsp smoked paprika
3 Tomatoes, diced
1 Bunch fresh basil, chopped
2 Small cans no sugar added tomato paste
1 Cup water
2 Tsp Swerve
1 Tbs Pink Himalayan Salt
2 Tsp black pepper
5 Tbs mild olive oil

Servings: 8 - 10

Shakshuka

1. Using a medium to large 2 inch deep stove-top pan, heat up the oil and then add the red pepper strips, sliced garlic, whole jalapeños, diced onion and tomato paste and sauté all together on a medium to high temperature for 10 minutes
2. Add diced tomatoes to pan mixture and cook for another 5 minutes
3. Add 1/3 cup water and the paprika, salt, and pepper
4. Cover and let cook 10 minutes
5. Using a spatula, make a hole for each individual egg and gently place inside
6. Cover and cook for 5 minutes
7. Sprinkle Feta cheese on the top and garnish with parsley
8. Cover and let finish to cook for 10 minutes

Ingredients:

1 large red bell pepper,
        cut into thin strips
4 Whole Jalapeños
7 Garlic cloves, peeled
        and cut into slices
10 Tomatoes Peeled and diced
1 large onion, diced
1/4 Cup chopped parsley
8 Eggs
2 Tbs Tomato paste
1/4 Cup Feta cheese
1 Mounted Tbs Paprika
1 Tsp of Himalayan salt
1/4 Tsp Black pepper
1/4 Cup Coconut oil

Servings: 4

Raw Zucchini Lasagna

Macadamia Cheese:
1. Soak the raw macadamia nuts in 4 cups of water for at least 7 hours. You can let them soak overnight
2. Drain the nuts and rinse them off with warm water
3. Put all ingredients in blender or food processor
4. Add 1 cup of water and pulse on and off
5. You want it to have the consistency of cream cheese
6. Add a bit more water / lemon juice as needed
7. Store in refrigerator

Assembly:
These are assembled for individual layers not in a pan
1. Take 1 or 2 strips of zucchini
2. Top with some macadamia cheese
3. Add some pili pesto
4. Add some tomato sauce
5. Add a whole slice of homegrown tomato
6. Repeat for 2 more layers
7. Top with brain octane oil
8. Acknowledge round of applause when you serve it.
Freezes well. Improves with age.

Ingredients:

Macadamia Cheese:
2 cups raw macadamia nuts
3-4 tablespoons of lemon juice
1 teaspoon of Himalayan salt
pinch of garlic powder
pinch of white pepper
(optional) 1/2-1 teaspoon of stevia

Pili Nut Pesto:
2 cups of fresh basil leaves
2 whole garlic cloves
3/4 cup pili nuts
1/2 cup of extra virgin olive oil
1 teaspoon of lemon juice
1/4 teaspoon of Himalayan salt
pinch of black pepper

Tomato Oregano Sauce:
4 large raw tomatoes (crush in food processor but do not liquify)
1 tablespoon of oregano (fresh if you can get it)
1 tablespoon of apple cider vinegar
1 teaspoon of Himalayan salt
1 teaspoon black pepper

Zucchini Noodles:
Using your mandolin cut thin even strips of zucchini

Sliced Homegrown Tomatoes

Servings: 6

Shutterstock / Chef Christopher Slawson

CompletelyKeto

Side Dishes

Creamy Mashed Cauliflower

1. Wash & cut up cauliflower into 1/4 pieces
2. Cook in a small pan with 1 cup water until tender
3. Drain well
4. Using a food processor place cauliflower, cream, butter, sour cream, salt, pepper & minced garlic
5. Pulse until smooth & creamy
6. Serve hot in a bowl and garnish with chives and a slice of butter

Ingredients:

1 Head of cauliflower
6 Tbs heavy cream
3 Tbs butter
4 Tbs sour cream
1/4 Tsp black pepper
1 Tbs freshly chopped chives
1 Tsp Pink Himalayan salt
1/2 Tsp minced garlic

Servings: 6

Shutterstock / Brent Hofacker

Creamed Spinach

1. Melt butter in a large pan
2. Pour in heavy cream, stirring constantly
3. Add cream cheese
4. Pour broth in pan and cook until hot, on a medium-low flame
5. Add salt, pepper and minced garlic
6. Stir in spinach until heated through
7. Simmer over low heat for 7-10 minutes
8. Serve warm

Ingredients:

1/2 Cup butter
5 Oz cream cheese
1 Cup heavy cream
2 Cups Vegetable broth,
    or broth of choice
18 Ounces frozen spinach,
    thawed & drained well
2 Tsp Pink Himalayan salt
1 1/2 Tsp black pepper
4 Large garlic cloves, minced

Servings: 8

Shutterstock / zkruger

Cranberry Sauce

1. Bring water and Xylitol to boil in a medium pot
2. Place cranberries inside the pot after it has come to a rolling boil
3. Return water and cranberries to a boil
4. Reduce the heat and boil lightly for 10-15 minutes
5. Stir every minute
6. Remove from heat and cover
7. Allow to cool and place in refrigerator until ready to serve

Ingredients:

1 Cup water
1 Cup Xylitol
10 oz cranberries fresh/frozen

Servings: 6

Note:

Other Keto sweeteners will not work with this recipe.

Yapchik

1. In a 9 x 12 pan position minute steaks side by side covering the bottom
2. Place minute steaks in oven on 350 degrees for 45 minutes
3. Chop 2 onions into small squares and saute in a pan until golden
4. When steaks are ready remove from the oven and spread golden onions evenly over the steaks
5. Whisk the eggs by hand with a whisker very quickly, and then add the salt and pepper
6. Whisk again until it turns into a bubbly liquid
7. In a food processor grate 1 onion and add to egg mixture
8. Remove any large pieces that did not get cut up
9. Add thawed and drained riced cauliflower to egg mixture and mix well
10. In a small pot heat up oil
11. Add hot oil to mixture and stir quickly with a large spoon
12. Pour mixture over the steak and onions and flatten out with a spatula and bake on 375 for 2 hours until it gets golden brown on top
13. If you like it more crispy on the outside start on 400 for the first hour and 375 for the 2nd hour until golden and crispy on top
14. Allow to cool for a few minutes and cut using a sharp knife

Ingredients:

6 Large minute steaks
    or 8 small minute steaks
3 Extra large yellow
    sweet onions
3 12 Oz packages of riced
    cauliflower defrosted
    and liquid removed
10 eggs
1 Tbs fine sea salt
1 Tsp Black pepper
1/2 Cup avocado oil

Servings: 16 - 20

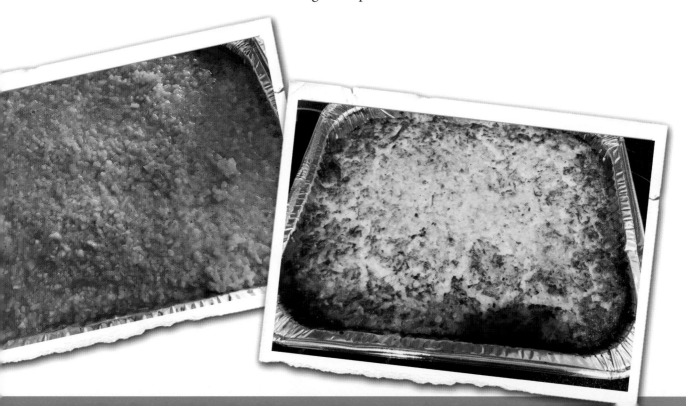

Baked Cauliflower Florets

1. Preheat oven to 425
2. Cover 2 large cookie sheets with parchment paper. Set aside
3. Pull cauliflower floret pieces apart, either by hand or using a knife creating small bite size pieces
4. In a platter or shallow bowl mix 1 cup almond flour, 1/2 tsp salt and 1/2 tsp black pepper and mix well
5. Dip each floret into the flour mixture
6. Beat eggs well in another bowl
7. Dip the floured florets into the beaten eggs
8. Place on prepared parchment lined cookie sheets
9. Sprinkle with salt & pepper
10. Put in oven for 20-25 minutes
11. In a small skillet melt the butter, stir in 1/4 cup flour, lemon juice, wine, and stock
12. Sprinkle 1/4 tsp salt and 1/4 tsp pepper
13. Bring to a simmer and allow to cook 3 minutes
14. Stir in parsley
15. Cool off in a small dipping bowl and serve on the side as a dip for the baked florets
16. Garnish with fresh pieces of parsley

Ingredients:

2 Heads cauliflower
1 1/4 Cups blanched almond flour
Pink Himalayan Salt
Ground black pepper
5 Eggs
4 Tbs butter
Juice of 1 lemon
1 Cup Pinot Grigio
1/2 Cup vegetable stock
        (tomato base or other)
6 Tbs chopped fresh curly parsley

Servings: 12

Paula's Mock Sweet Potato And Toasted Pecans

1. Preheat oven to 350
2. Lightly butter a 13 x 9 casserole
3. Toast pecans at 350 on a baking sheet covered with parchment paper and roast 7-10 minutes
4. Set aside pecans to cool then chop
5. Cut cauliflower into florets and steam until soft
6. Drain cauliflower then, remove all excess moisture by squeezing in cheesecloth
7. Put the cauliflower in a food processor and blend until creamy
8. Then, set aside
9. In a large bowl beat eggs and yolk with butter, Swerve and Lakanto Syrup
10. Add pumpkin, heavy cream, vanilla, cinnamon, and salt to the egg mixture
11. Now add your creamy cauliflower and mix all together and pour your mixture into the greased casserole

Crumble Topping:
1. Add Swerve and Lakanto Syrup to melted butter and mix
2. Mix Almond flour, cinnamon and toasted, chopped pecans together
3. Then add to butter mixture
4. Combine all the ingredients together with a fork to create a crumble
5. Disperse the Crumble Topping over the Mock Sweet Potato
6. Bake at 350 degrees for 35-45 minutes

Ingredients:

Mock Sweet Potato:
1 1/4 Cup canned pumpkin, unsweetened
1 Large head cauliflower, should yield 3 cups
2 Eggs
1 Egg yolk
1/2 Cup heavy cream
5 Tbs Melted butter
1/4 Cup Swerve
2 Tsp Lakanto Syrup
1 Tsp Vanilla
1/2 Tsp cinnamon
1/2 Tsp Pink Himalayan Salt

Crumble Topping:
1/2 Tsp cinnamon
4-5 Tbs melted butter
1/2 Cup Swerve
1/2 Cup plus 1 tbs almond flour
1 Cup toasted pecans
1 Tsp Lakanto Syrup

Servings: 8

Mushroom and Celery Stuffing

1. Using the croutonz or bunz cut up from Fox Hill Kitchens
2. Soak in hot water until soft and squeeze out water
3. Heat oil or fat in skillet
4. Add celery, onion and mushrooms and cook for about 7 minutes on a low-medium heat
5. Pour over softened bread and mix
6. Add eggs, and seasonings to bread mixture
7. Stuff poultry (enough for 5-6 pound turkey, duck or chicken)
8. If any leftover, place in a greased oven-proof dish and bake in oven at the same time basting with the drippings

Ingredients:

4 Cups Fox Hill Kitchens Croutonz or Bunz cut up
1/4 Cup Coconut oil or chicken fat
1/2 Cup onion, finely diced
3/4 Cup diced celery
1 Cup Portabella mushrooms, finely chopped
2 Eggs beaten well
1/8 Tsp black pepper
1 Tsp poultry seasoning
1 Tsp Pink Himalayan Salt

Servings: 6

Shutterstock / Brent Hofacker

Mock "Potato" Kugel

1. Preheat oven to 400
2. Whisk the eggs by hand with a whisker very quickly, and then add the salt and pepper
3. Whisk again until it turns into a bubbly liquid
4. In a food processor grate 1 onion and add to egg mixture
5. Remove any large pieces that did not get cut up
6. Add thawed and drained riced cauliflower to egg mixture and mix well
7. In a small pot heat up oil
8. Add hot oil to mixture and stir quickly with a large spoon
9. Pour mixture into 3 small greased loaf pans
10. Bake for 1 1/2 hours or until golden in color

Ingredients:

3 12 Oz packages of cauliflower rice thawed and liquid squeezed out by hand

10 eggs

1 Tbs sea salt

1 Tsp black pepper

1/2 Cup Coconut or olive oil or butter

1 Large onion

3 small loaf pans, greased well with butter or oil

Servings: 17

Holiday Sausage Stuffing

1. Preheat oven to 350
2. Saute onion and celery in a frying pan with 3 Tbs of oil or butter
3. Season with the salt and pepper and cook for about 10 minutes on a medium to low temperature
4. Add the mushrooms and cook for 5 minutes
5. Add the rest of the oil or butter
6. Add the sausage sliced into 1/4 inch cut up pieces, along with the chopped parsley and cook for 7 minutes on a medium temperature
7. Transfer mixture to a large bowl and toss in the Fox Hill Kitchens Croutonz
8. Mix in the eggs and broth over stuffing and let sit for 2 minutes and toss again
9. Pour into a lightly greased ceramic baking dish
10. Place in the oven covered for 20 minutes
11. Remove cover and bake 10 minutes or until browned and crisp on the top
12. This recipe can be baked ahead of time and reheated for a few minutes before serving

Ingredients:

1.5 Pounds of Sausage
(no sugar added)
1 Bag Fox Hill Kitchens
Croutonz
1 Onion, diced
4 Ribs of celery, sliced thin
1 Bunch of fresh parsley,
finely chopped
6 Tbs Olive oil, butter or
coconut oil
2 Eggs, beaten
2 Tsp Pink Himalayan Salt
1 1/2 Tsp black pepper
1 Cup Chicken or
vegetable broth
8 Oz Portabella mushrooms
coarsely chopped

Servings: 16 - 20

Broccoli Pudding

1. Preheat oven to 350
2. Thoroughly wash broccoli and trim off any tough ends
3. Cook in a pot until tender but not too soft
4. Drain well and mash well in a mixer / food processor
5. Combine in a small 1 1/2 quart saucepan the butter or oil, coconut milk and flour
6. Simmer over a low flame and then allow to cool for about 5 minutes
7. In a large bowl with the mashed broccoli add the mayonnaise, eggs, onion powder, salt and pepper and mix well
8. Add the cooled mixture from the pan and mix well
9. Grease a 9 x 12 Pyrex or porcelain oven safe pan
10. Fill in with broccoli mixture and spread evenly
11. Bake for 30 minutes or until golden
12. After about 10-15 minutes of baking, open the oven and poke some fork holes around

Ingredients:

1 Large bunch broccoli
1 1/2 Tbs butter or coconut oil
1 1/2 Tbs Almond flour
1/2 Cup Unsweetened
     Coconut milk
1/2 Cup Primal Kitchen
     Mayonnaise
3 Eggs beaten
1 Tsp Pink Himalayan Salt
Black Pepper to taste
1 Tbs onion powder

Servings: 12

Cauliflower "Mac" and Cheese Casserole

1. Preheat oven to 375 degrees F. Bring a large pot of water to a boil. Season the water with salt
2. Coat the pan with coconut oil or olive oil
3. Cook the cauliflower in the boiling water until crisp-tender, about 5 minutes.
4. Drain well and pat between several layers of paper towels to dry. Transfer the cauliflower to the baking dish and set aside
5. Whisk in the cream cheese and mustard until smooth.
6. Stir in 1 cup of the cheese, salt, pepper and garlic and whisk just until the cheese melts, about 1 to 2 minutes.
7. Remove from heat, pour over the cauliflower, and stir to combine.
8. Top with the remaining 1/2 cup cheese and bake until browned and bubbly hot, about 15 minutes.

Ingredients:

Kosher salt, as needed,
    plus 1/2 teaspoon
1 large head cauliflower,
    cut into small florets
Vegetable oil spray
2 ounces cream cheese,
    cut into small pieces
1 1/2 teaspoons Dijon mustard
1 1/2 cups shredded sharp
    Cheddar, plus 1/2 cup for
    topping the casserole
1/4 teaspoon freshly ground
    black pepper
1/8 teaspoon garlic powder

Servings: 8 - 10

Roasted Red Peppers

1. Turn broiler on low and place red peppers on a large metal tray
2. Put in broiler for 2-3 minutes on each side as you finish all 3 sides of pepper
3. Remove from broiler and let cool 5 minutes
4. Using caution peel the skin off of the flesh of the pepper and remove stem and some seeds
5. Using a cutting board slice peppers into 1 inch long slices
6. Preheat oven to 250
7. Line parchment paper on large metal tray about 12 x 18 inches
8. Place sliced peppers on the tray and set aside
9. Mix together the sliced garlic, vinegar, olive oil and salt
10. Drizzle evenly over peppers
11. Put tray in center of oven for 20 minutes and turn over and again for another 20 minutes
12. Continue to watch until begins to dry
13. Serve as appetizer or side dish

Ingredients:

8 Large Red Peppers
1 Tbs Apple Cider Vinegar
2 Tbs Olive Oil
1 Tsp Pink Himalayan Salt
6 Cloves Fresh Garlic,
    sliced thin

Servings: 12

Wok Stir-Fried String Beans

1. Heat up wok on medium-high heat
2. Cut ends off and clean string beans
3. Toss into wok
4. Drizzle oil all over evenly and toss
5. Pour wheat free tamari, garlic powder & black pepper and toss constantly for 3-5 minutes
6. If you enjoy a more crispy string bean then let it cook only 3 minutes
7. If you enjoy a more well done blackened flavor, allow to cook closer to 5 minutes
8. Optional:
9. If desired add lemon slices about a minute before removing from the wok

Ingredients:

12 Oz (340 Grams) string beans
3 Tbs Coconut oil or olive oil
2 Tbs Wheat free tamari
2 Tsp garlic powder
1 Tsp ground black pepper
Lemon slices cut in halves
    (optional)

Servings: 6

Jicama French Fries

1. Gently mix all above ingredients together
2. Add Mixture to Air Fryer
3. Set timer for 15 minutes
4. When the bell rings, dig in!

Ingredients:

Jicama sticks
extra virgin olive oil to cover
Spices to taste:
Salt
pepper
garlic powder
onion powder
smokey paprika

Servings: 12

Helpful Hint:

Perfect with homemade ketchup! Find the recipe on page 156.

I Can't Believe It's Not Potato Latkes

1. Using fresh or frozen riced cauliflower, heat up a skillet with some oil on the bottom and add riced cauliflower to the skillet
2. Saute until well cooked, stirring occasionally for about 5 -7 minutes on medium-low and set aside
3. Cut the onion into 6 pieces and place in food processor, leaving the onions smooth and having no large pieces
4. Add onion to the cooked cauliflower and mix well
5. In a bowl, whisk 4 eggs together with a beater until well beaten
6. Add the cooked riced cauliflower and onion mix to the bowl and stir
7. Add the salt, pepper, and xanthan gum and mix well
8. In an electric fryer or deep skillet, heat up oil until bubbling slightly
9. Using an ice cream scoop or a measuring cup of 1/4 cup size drop the mixture into the oil, never frying too many too closely
10. Leave space in between, as they will spread in size
11. Fry until golden in color
12. Remove and place onto a prepared plate of paper towels to drain excess oil
13. Serve on a plate with a Tablespoon of Sour Cream at it's side

Ingredients:

2 12 Oz Packages of
          cauliflower rice
1   Large Vidalia onion
4 Large eggs beaten well
1 Heaping tsp of Xanthan Gum
1 Flat Tbs iodized sea salt
1/2 Tsp black pepper
Mild Olive oil or Avocado oil
          for frying
Serve with sour cream on the side

Servings: 12

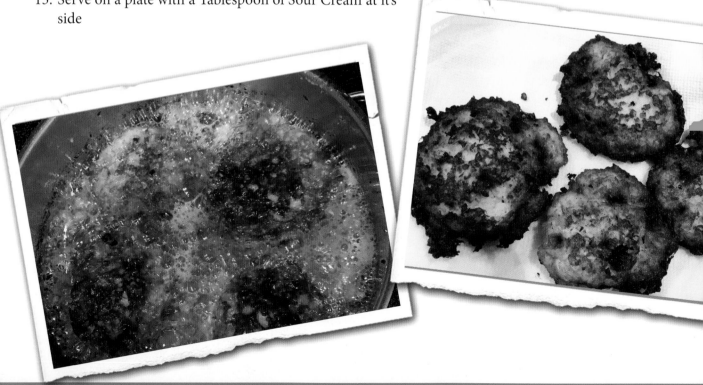

Shirataki Vegetable Lo Mein

1. Prepare Shirataki noodles and set aside
2. Prepare seasoning mix in a small bowl and set aside
3. Heat up a wok or a saute pan
4. Saute all vegetables over high heat, for about 2-4 minutes
5. Add Shirataki noodles and seasoning mixture and stir

Ingredients:

2 7 Ounce packages of Shirataki
       Spaghetti
1 Carrot, shredded
1 1/2 Cups shredded red cabbage
3 Oz sliced mushrooms
2 Scallions, chopped small
1 Cup string beans, cut up
6 Oz broccoli, chopped
1/2 Red pepper, sliced into strips
1/2 Orange pepper into strips
1 Zucchini, diced

Seasoning:
5 Tsp Wheat-free tamari
2 Tsp Swerve
3 Cloves garlic minced
2 Tsp fresh minced ginger

Garnish:
1/4 Cup fresh chopped parsley

Servings: 4

Air Fryer Zucchini Fries

1. Set Air Fryer to 380 degrees
2. Using a large bowl, mix coconut flour, parsley, parmesan, salt, pepper, garlic & basil
3. Set aside
4. Pour almond flour in a small bowl
5. Beat eggs well in a separate bowl
6. Dip zucchini sticks first into almond flour, then beaten eggs and end off with dipping into coconut flour spice mixture
7. Place coated zucchini fries one by one into air fryer as they are ready and completely coated
8. Cook in air fryer for 20 minutes
9. Serve with some sour cream on the side

Ingredients:

1 Cup coconut flour
3/4 Cup grated parmesan
    cheese
1 Tsp Pink Himalayan Salt
1 Tsp basil
1 Tsp garlic powder
1/2 Tsp black pepper
3 Tbs fresh parsley, chopped
3 Eggs
1/2 Cup Blanched almond flour
4 Medium zucchini,
    cut into 3 inch sticks
Sour cream on the side

Servings: 8

Italian Oven-Dried Tomatoes

These delicious oven-dried tomatoes can be added to salads for more flavor, omelettes, or just enjoy as a snack with some sliced cheese on the go.

1. Preheat oven to 250
2. Line a large pan with parchment paper
3. Slice each tomato in half lengthwise
4. Gently squeeze out excess liquid
5. Place tomatoes on tray in rows
6. Drizzle olive oil onto each tomato
7. Grind fresh black pepper over generously
8. Sprinkle with coarse ground pink Himalayan salt
9. Top with dry basil
10. Rub in minced garlic
11. Place in oven between 4-6 hours depending on your preference
12. Remove from oven
13. Allow to cool
14. Store in airtight container in the refrigerator

Ingredients:

12 Ripe plum tomatoes
6 Cloves finely minced fresh garlic
Fresh ground black pepper
2 Tsp dry basil
Olive oil
Coarse Pink Himalayan Salt

Servings: 24

CompletelyKeto

Breads

Lemon Zucchini Bread

1. Preheat Oven to 350 degrees
2. Butter a loaf pan
3. Combine all dry ingredients
4. Add egg, butter, lemon juice, lemon peel
5. Stir only with a spatula
6. Drain the liquid from the zucchini
7. Add zucchini and stir well
8. Place in oven
9. Bake for only 45-50 minutes

Ingredients:

1/2 of a cup grass fed butter
2 eggs
1/4 tsp of pink
      Himalayan salt
1/4 tsp baking powder
1/2 tsp baking soda
1/2 cup Swerve or Xylitol
2 Tbs lemon juice
2 Tbs finely diced lemon peel
1 cup shredded fresh zucchini
3/4 cup of extra fine
      almond flour
1/4 cup of coconut flour

Servings: 6 - 8

Tsippy Kilstein's Nearly World Famous Keto Rolls

1. Preheat oven to 350 degrees
2. In a Vitamix or Cuisinart, pulse together tahini and eggs until very smooth
3. Add in apple cider vinegar and swerve
4. Add the baking soda and salt
5. Transfer batter to pan greased with coconut oil
6. Bake at 350° for 35 – 45 minutes depending on your oven
7. Makes 6 large muffins or 12 small muffins. These rise so fill the tin only half way. You can also make them in a loaf pan.

Ingredients:

1 cup whole tahini butter
        (from ground sesame)
5 large eggs
1 tablespoon apple cider
        vinegar
2 Tbs swerve
¾ Tsp baking soda
¼ Tsp Himalayan
        Pink Salt

Servings: 6

Almond Rolls

1. Preheat oven to 350 degrees
2. In a Vitamix or Cuisinart, pulse together almond butter and eggs until very smooth
3. Add in apple cider vinegar and swerve
4. Add the baking soda and salt
5. Transfer batter to pan greased with coconut oil
6. Bake at 350° for 35 – 45 minutes depending on your oven
7. Top each roll with an almond
8. Makes 6 large muffins or 12 small muffins. These rise so fill the tin only half way. You can also make them in a loaf pan.

Ingredients:

1 cup almond butter (no sugar)
5 large eggs
1 Tbs apple cider vinegar
2 Tbs swerve
¾ tsp baking soda
¼ tsp Himalayan Pink Salt
12 Whole almonds

Servings: 6 - 12

New York Style Pretzels: Salty or Sweet

1. Preheat oven to 400
2. Mix the shredded cheese and almond flour in a microwaveable bowl
3. Add the cream cheese and stir
4. Microwave for 1 minute
5. Stir again
6. Then microwave for another 30 seconds
7. Add the eggs and combine well together
8. Separate the dough into 4 equal parts
9. Grease 2 sheets of parchment paper using butter generously on two separate baking pans
10. On a work surface, make 4 long rolled out rods
11. Create 4 individual pretzel twisted designs
12. Place two Pretzel twists on one sheet and bake in oven for 15 minutes
13. Remove from oven and wet your fingers and rub moisture all over pretzels
14. As soon as you can after that, sprinkle Pretzel Salt all over generously (If you use regular salt it absorbs into the dough, the Pretzel Salt is made to just stay on the surface of the pretzel)
15. Place in oven for another few minutes watching it to not get burned
16. Place the other two pretzel twists on the other baking sheet
17. Sprinkle with cinnamon and Swerve
18. Bake in oven between 10- 20 minutes

Ingredients:

Pretzel Dough:
3 1/2 cups pre shredded mozzarella cheese
1 1/2 cups almond flour
4 tbsp cream cheese
2 eggs

Salty Pretzels:
Pretzel Salt

Sweet Pretzels:
1 Tsp Swerve Granular Sweetener
1 Tsp Cinnamon

Servings: 12

CompletelyKeto

Sauces & Rubs

Tahini Sauce

Combine all ingredients in a blender
Combine until the consistency you like.
Some people like it a little thicker.
Some people like it a little thinner.
What works best for you?
This is a great fat to add to all salads.

Ingredients:

1 cup whole tahini
1/2 Tsp Pink Himalayan salt
1/4 Tsp Pepper
2 cloves fresh garlic
1/4 cup of lemon juice
3/4 cup water
Sprig of parsley to garnish

Servings: 8

Shutterstock /

Make Your Mouth Smile BBQ Rub

Combine all ingredients together in a bowl and coat meat with rub, then let it sit before grilling or smoking.

Ingredients:

4 tblsp garlic powder
2 tblsp onion powder
2 tblsp smoked paprika
2 tblsp Spanish Paprika
1/2 tsp sumac
2 tsp dried oregano
4 tblsp chilli power
1 tsp. white pepper
1/2 tsp cayenne pepper
2 tsp kosher salt
2 tsp xylitol or swerve

Servings: 4

Shutterstock /

Secret Memphis BBQ Sauce

1. Gently mix all above ingredients together
2. Simmer on low heat for 20 minutes at least
3. Refrigerate

Ingredients:

2 cups Sugar Free Tomato sauce
2 DROPS Sugar Free Liquid Smoke
    (I use Lazy Kettle)
2/3 cup Apple cider vinegar
1 tblsp Bourbon
2/3 cup Lakanto, Xylitol, or Swerve
2 tbs coconut oil
1 tbs deli mustard
1 Onion, medium, finely chopped
2 Garlic cloves, minced
2 tblsp Chili powder
1/2 tsp ground Black pepper
1/2 tsp cumin
1/2 tsp fresh oregano
1 leaf fresh basil minced
1 tsp sugar free hot sauce

Servings: 4

Homemade Ketchup

1. Mix all ingredients in a small pot
2. Stir on low heat for a few minutes
3. Allow to cool
4. Store in a jar in refrigerator

Ingredients:

6 oz can of Tomato paste
1 1/2 Tbs Apple cider vinegar
1 Tbs Swerve Granular Sweetener
3/4 Tsp Pink Himalayan Salt
3/4 Tsp granulated garlic
3/4 Tsp granulated onion
1/8 Tsp allspice
1/2 Tbs Lakanto syrup
1/16 Tsp cayenne pepper
2/3 Cup water
1/2 Tsp Xanthan Gum

Servings: 14

Shutterstock / Sergey Lapin

Do It Yourself Dill Tartar Sauce

1. Put all ingredients into a food processor and pulse a couple times until well combined
2. Store in a jar in the refrigerator for a couple days

Ingredients:

1 Cup Primal Kitchen Mayo
5 Tbs Fresh dill finely chopped
1 1/2 Tsp fresh lemon zest
4 Medium no sugar added dill pickles or 2 large chopped into small cubes
3/4 Tsp Pink Himalayan Salt
3/4 Tsp black pepper

Yields: 2 Cups

Shutterstock / Louno Morose

Shutterstock / Vladislav Noseek

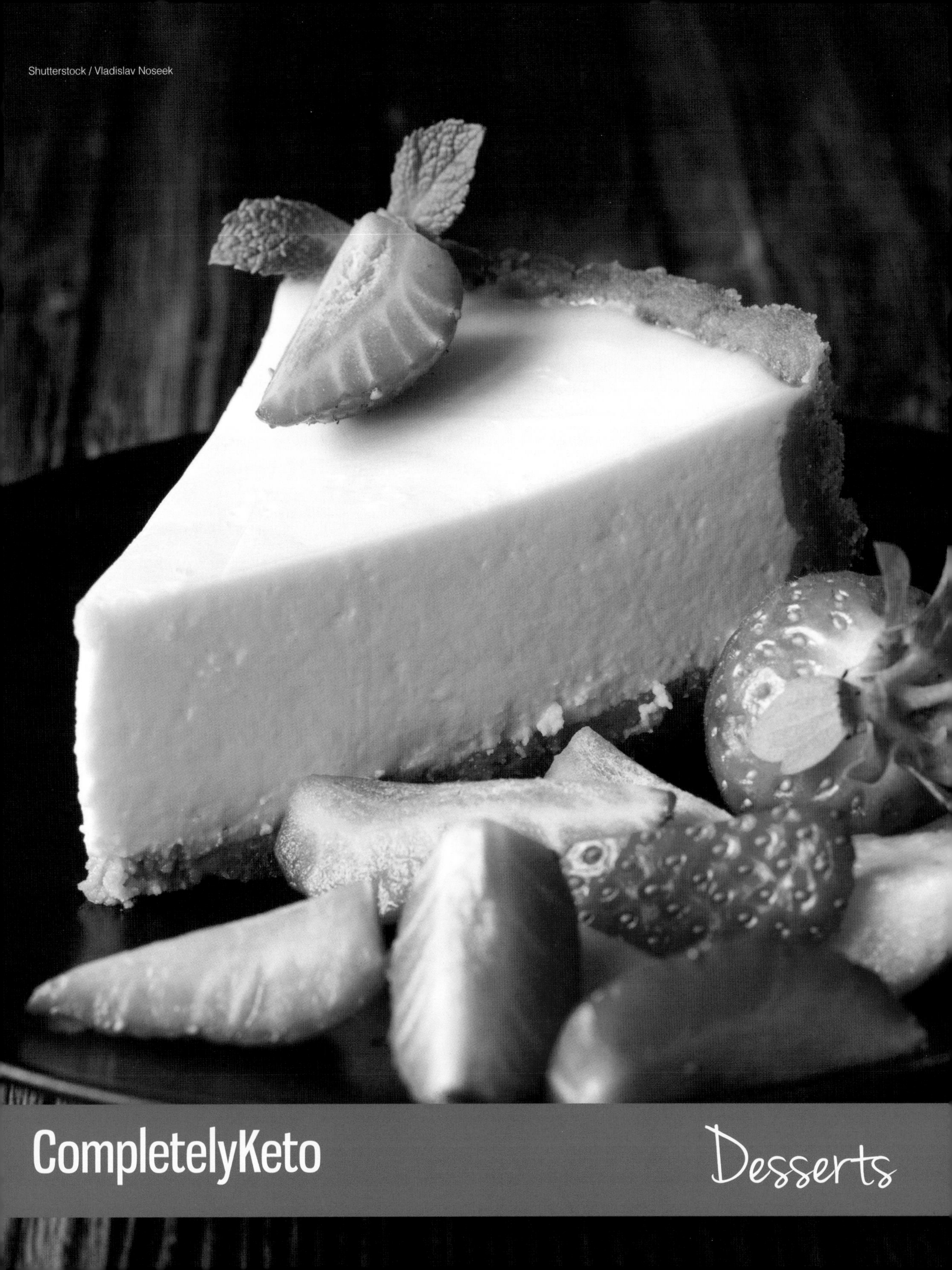

CompletelyKeto Desserts

Keto-Friendly Drinks

Berry Cocktail:
1. In a small pan, mix together Swerve and water and bring to a boil
2. Allow to cool
3. Place in refrigerator for 30 minutes
4. Place berries in glass and press down with a wooden spoon
5. Fill glass halfway with ice
6. Add lime juice, vodka and cooled Swerve mix and stir
7. Splash some Zevia Ginger Ale
8. Drop sprig of Rosemary on the side

Ingredients:

Berry Cocktail:
1/4 Cup Swerve
1/4 Cup Water
3 Raspberries
5 Blueberries
2 Blackberries
1 Sprig fresh Rosemary
Ice
1/4 Lime, Squeezed
1/4 Cup Vodka
Zevia Ginger Ale

Rum & Cola:
1 Can Zevia Cola
1/4 Cup Rum of choice
Lime Wedges
Ice

Mojito:
1/2 Oz Squeezed Fresh Lime Juice
1 Tsp Swerve
5 Mint leaves
2 1/2 Oz White Rum
Splash of Lime Zevia Sparkling Water

Shutterstock / 5PH

Rum & Cola:
1. Mix Rum and Zevia Cola
2. Add Ice Cubes
3. Mix well
4. Add slices of Lime Wedges

Mojito:
1. Mix Lime Juice with Swerve
2. Add Mint Leaves
3. Press the leaves against the wall of the glass and then mix quickly using a wooden spoon
4. Fill glass up to 1/2 with ice and pour in rum
5. Splash the end with Lime Zevia Sparkling Water

Gingerbread Cookies

1. Mix all ingredients together starting with the eggs and ending with all of the dry ingredients
2. Place dough in refrigerator for about an hour or so
3. Preheat oven to 275
4. Cut two sheets of parchment paper
5. Place half of dough in between the two pieces of parchment and roll out to desired thickness between 1/4 inch and 1/2 inch thick
6. Choose cookie cutter shapes and cut out desired amount of each
7. Repeat with the other half of the dough
8. If you have leftover dough, roll out again and cut again using cookie cutter shape
9. Lay cookies on parchment paper or cookie mat
10. Bake in oven for about 25 minutes until lightly golden
11. Remove from the oven and cool on rack
12. Using a powdered sugar sifter, sprinkle the Swerve confectioners over the cookies
13. Store in an airtight container

Ingredients:

1 1/2 Cups almond flour
1/3 Cup Swerve Granular
1/3 Cup Swerve Confectioners
3 Extra large eggs
1/3 Cup butter
1/4 Tsp sea salt
1 Tsp baking powder
1 Tbs pumpkin pie spice
1 Tsp powdered ginger
1 Tsp cinnamon

Yields: 30 - 40 cookies

Shutterstock / Maximov Denis

Shutterstock / Timolina

Drop Down Chocolate Chip Cookies

1. Heat oven to 350
2. Grease Baking Trays and line with parchment paper
3. Using a large mixing bowl, combine flour, baking soda and salt and set aside
4. In the cake mixer beat the butter for about a minute, add sugar and beat for 2-3 minutes until fluffy
5. On a low speed combine the eggs, vanilla and 4 Tbs water and mix well
6. Add flour gradually until combined, ending with the chocolate chips
7. Using a Tablespoon as a measurement place balls of dough 1 inch apart from each other.
8. Then, place tray in freezer between 15-18 minutes before baking
9. Place tray in oven to bake for 10 minutes while preparing the 2nd tray of cookies
10. When the 10 minutes are up, open oven and lift baking tray and drop it down onto the oven rack so the center of the cookies drop down. If necessary drop twice
11. Repeat every 2-3 minutes until cookies are golden brown on the edges, soft in the center and spread out in size.
12. Bake 16-18 minutes total
13. Since all ovens are different, watch your cookies carefully so they don't burn
14. Allow to cool before removing from baking tray

Ingredients:

12 Ounces Lilly's chocolate chips
3 Tsps Pure Vanilla Extract
4 Cups Almond Flour
2 Eggs
1 Tsp Baking soda
1 1/2 Tsps Pink Himalayan Salt
1 Pound unsalted butter /4 sticks butter room temperature
1 1/2 Cups Swerve Granular Sweetener

Yields: 40 - 50 cookies

Chocolate Chocolate Chip Cookies

1. Preheat Oven to 350 degrees
2. Cream together butter, xylitol or swerve, and Lakanto golden
3. add heavy whipped cream and vanilla extract, baking soda
4. add coconut flour and cocoa
5. add almond flour 1/4 of a cup at a time and mix
6. stir in pecan pieces and chocolate chips
7. form 18 cookies
8. Please note, in the summer refrigerate the dough for an hour or freeze it for a half-hour
9. Place in oven on greased cookie sheet
10. Bake for only 8-10 minutes. The cookies should be perfect.
11. Cool on a wire rack

Ingredients:

1 1/2 cups of super fine almond flour
1/4 cup of coconut flour
1/4 teaspoon baking soda
2 tablespoons of heavy whipped cream
1 cup (2 sticks) grass fed butter, softened
1 cup swerve or xylitol
1/2 cup Lakanto golden sweetener
1 teaspoon Rodelle vanilla extract
1/3 cup unsweetened cocoa
1 cup broken pecans
1 cups Lilly's Chocolate chips

Helpful Hint:

The balance of the two flours and the two sweeteners is important for consistency. If you have a nut allergy and use all coconut flour, it's going to be dry. If you hate coconut and want to use all almond flour try adding an extra 1/4 cup. For best results, follow the recipe.

Yields: 18 cookies

Cookie Monster Chocolate Chip Cookies

1. Preheat Oven to 375 degrees
2. Cream together butter, swerve, and Lakanto golden
3. add eggs and vanilla extract, salt, baking soda
4. add coconut flour
5. add almond flour 1/4 of a cup at a time and mix
6. form 18 cookies
7. Please note, especially in the summer, refrigerate the dough for an hour or freeze it for half an hour
8. Place in oven on greased cookie sheet
9. Bake for only 8-10 minutes
10. The cookies should be perfect
11. Cool on a wire rack

Ingredients:

2 cups of super fine almond flour
1/4 cup of coconut flour
1 teaspoon baking soda
1 teaspoon of pink Himalayan salt
1 cup (2 sticks) grass fed butter, softened
3/4 cup swerve or xylitol
3/4 cup Lakanto golden sweetener
1 teaspoon Rodelle vanilla extract
2 large eggs
2 cups Lilly's Chocolate chips

Yields: 18 cookies

Helpful Hint:

The balance of the two flours and the two sweeteners is important for consistency. If you have a nut allergy and use all coconut flour, it's going to be dry. If you hate coconut and want to use all almond flour try adding an extra 1/4 cup. For best results, follow the recipe.

Banana Custard

1. Blend 2 3/4 cups water in a blender with 2 Tbs Tahini
2. Place in a pot
3. Add banana extract and pinch of salt
4. Stir well on medium-low heat
5. Add Agar and stir
6. Add vanilla, swerve and lemon zest and keep stirring
7. Bring heat up to a medium flame and allow to come to a boil , stirring constantly
8. Cook for a few minutes
9. Remove from heat and pour into individual custard ramekins and then cool in refrigerator for a couple hours
10. Serve garnished with choice berries and a leaf of mint

Ingredients:

5 Tsp Banana extract
2 Tbs Tahini
2 3/4 cups water
1/2 Tbs Agar Agar
2 Tsp vanilla
1 1/2 Tsp fresh lemon zest
1/4 Tsp cinnamon
2 Tbs Swerve
Pinch of salt
Garnish: blueberries,
          raspberries,
          strawberries,
          and a leaf of mint

Servings: 8 - 10

Strawberry & "Apple" Sauce

1. In a medium sauce pot bring water to a boil
2. Add chopped zucchini and strawberries and mix together
3. Add Swerve, pinch of salt and cinnamon and stir
4. Cook for 15 minutes on low
5. Serve in mini bowls

Ingredients:

4 Zucchini, peeled and chopped
          into very small triangles
16 Ounces of strawberries,
          chopped small
4 Tbs Swerve Granular
1 1/2 Cups water
Pinch of Pink Himalayan Salt
1 Tsp cinnamon

Servings: 6 - 8

Strawberry Shortcake

1. Preheat oven to 350
2. In a cake mixer, combine the coconut flour, baking soda, eggs, butter, Lakanto and vanilla
3. Grease two 9 inch round pans with butter
4. Pour batter into both pans
5. Bake for 25-30 minutes or until a toothpick comes out clean in the center. All ovens vary in temperature so please check oven frequently from the outside door
6. Remove from oven and cool on cooling rack before filling & frosting the cake
7. In a mixer bowl, cream butter. Add Swerve confectioners sweetener, vanilla, salt, and enough Coconut milk or creamer to achieve a spreadable consistency.
8. Spread frosting on top of one cake sheet in between the two cakes and lay thin slices of strawberries evenly.
9. Place the other cake on top of the strawberries and frosting.
10. Frost the outside of the cake, evenly all around. When the frosting is done, decorate the top with strawberry slices .

Ingredients:

9 Extra large eggs
1/2 cup Lakanto Syrup
1 Tbs Vanilla Extract
3/4 Cup coconut flour
1/2 Tsp baking soda
1/2 Cup butter, salted & softened

Filling and Topping:
1 1/2 Pounds of fresh strawberries sliced thin
1/2 Cup melted butter
6 Cups Swerve Confectioners Sweetener
2 Tsps Vanilla Extract
Pinch of Pink Himalayan Salt
6-10 Tbs Unsweetened Coconut milk or creamer

Servings: 12

Shutterstock / YoloStock

Holiday Cranberry Scones

1. Wash cranberries and place in a bowl with boiling water and soak for 10 minutes, they should split open
2. Drain and dry in a towel, getting rid of as much moisture as possible
3. Mix the cranberries with a water and sweetener mixture of 1 cup water and 1/2 cup XyloSweet (For 12 Ounces of fresh cranberries you will only need 1/4 cup of this mixture)
4. Using a baking sheet covered in 2 sheets of parchment paper, place the cranberries spaced apart to allow air to circulate around
5. Set oven to 150 degrees
6. Place in oven for 8 hours, some like to do this step overnight
7. Remove and allow to cool for 15-30 minutes
8. Preheat oven to 350
9. Using cake beaters, combine the butter, Xylo Sweetener, egg and vanilla until fluffy
10. In a separate bowl, mix together the almond flour, baking soda and salt
11. Slowly combine both mixtures using a slow setting
12. By hand, add the dried cranberries and chopped almonds and mix well
13. Using an ice cream scooper drop scoopfuls of dough onto a greased baking tray spread apart
14. Bake 20-24 minutes depending on oven
15. Please check your scones carefully as every oven varies, when they just start to brown, remove
16. Allow to cool and place in an airtight container for storage

Ingredients:

2 1/2 Cups Fine Almond Flour
1 Tsp vanilla extract
3/4 Cup Xylo Sweet
1 Large egg
1 Cup Toasted slivered almonds, chopped coarsely
1/4 Tsp baking soda
1/4 Tsp kosher salt
1 Cup unsalted butter at room temperature
1 Cup dried cranberries

Yields: 24 scones

Helpful Hint:

Please keep in mind that the recipe calls for dried cranberries and the fresh cranberries will shrink in size, and this very important step in the recipe for sweet dried cranberries will help make the cranberries taste sweet like the ones that are packaged that you can buy at the store.

Frozen Raspberry Mousse

1. Using a mixer, whip up 3 egg whites
2. Set aside
3. Blend 2 cups of fresh or frozen raspberries. (If they are frozen be sure they aren't the ones with sugar in them)
4. Optional: add 1 tablespoon of vodka, rum, or tequila
5. Add 1/2 cup of Keto sweetener such as xylitol or swerve
6. Gently fold the egg whites into the batter using a large spoon
7. Minimally stir the egg whites and batter – the key word is minimally
8. Pour into glass bowl or container. I serve these in individual bowls with a raspberry and mint leaf on top

Ingredients:

3 egg whites
2 cups raspberries,
      fresh or frozen
1/2 cup xylitol or swerve

Servings: 4 - 6

Blackberry Muffins

1. Using a cupcake tray for 12 cupcakes and paper cup liners inside
2. Simmer butter over Medium-high heat until browned a bit
3. Mix all ingredients with your cake mixer
4. Spray paper liner cups
5. Fill each liner 3/4 with batter and drop 3 blackberries on top
6. Bake at 350 for 25 minutes or until golden
7. For the perfect muffin experience, serve warm

Ingredients:

1/2 Cup plus 5 Tbs unsalted butter

1 1/2 Cups Almond flour

1 1/2 Cups plus 2 Tbsp Swerve Confectioners

5 Egg whites

2 Tbs Lakanto Syrup

Nonstick spray

2 Cups blackberries

Servings: 12

Harlan Kilstein's Perfect Keto Cheesecake

This has quickly become the most popular cheesecake in keto - and there's a reason why. Make it once and you'll be hooked!

Crust:
1. Mix all ingredients together
2. Butter the springform pan
3. Press your mixture into the springform pan
4. Bake at 375 degrees for just 8 minutes

Filling:
1. **Leave all ingredients out for 6-8 hours to soften. This is a must!**
2. Beat the eggs and xylitol together
3. Add cream cheese, one tablespoon at a time until it's all creamy
4. Add the sour cream and vanilla
5. Add this mixture to your pie crust
6. Bake at 375 degrees for just 30 minutes
7. Now, turn off your oven and leave the cheesecake in the oven for one hour
8. Remove and refrigerate
9. Cover each slice with a single sliced strawberry or single blackberry

Ingredients:

Crust:
1 1/2 cup Almond Flour
1/2 cup melted grass-fed butter
1/4 cup xylitol (or other keto sweetener)
3/4 tsp cinnamon

Filling:
3 8 oz. packages of cream cheese
3 large eggs
16 oz. full fat sour cream
1 cup xylitol
1 tsp vanilla extract

Serves: 16

Toasted Pecan And Strawberry Mold

1. Place 8 oz bag of Pecans in a skillet on medium-low heat until toasted throughout stirring occasionally and chop on a cutting board into rough bits of pecan and set aside
2. Wash & cut up strawberries into small pieces and set aside
3. Use two pouches of the Simply Delish strawberry jel desserts in a glass bowl
4. Pour 2/3 cup cool water over the powder and stir until well dissolved
5. Using boiling water add 2 1/2 cups boiling water to the bowl and mix well
6. Add toasted pecan bits and strawberry pieces to strawberry liquid jel in glass bowl and stir until well combined
7. Pour entire mixture into 7 inch spring form bundt pan
8. Allow to cool for a few minutes and place in refrigerator
9. Sets in 1 hour and can be kept in fridge up to a few days prior to serving

Ingredients:

2 boxes 0.7 oz All natural Simply Delish Strawberry Jel Dessert
16 oz Strawberries
8 oz Toasted pecans

Servings: 16

Holiday "Honey" Cake

1. Preheat oven to 350 degrees
2. Combine all ingredients in mixing bowl or directly in Vita Mix
3. Gently mix and pour into greased loaf pan
4. Top with Toasted Slivered Almonds in design
5. Bake for 35-40 minutes until toothpick comes out clean

Ingredients:

2 2/3 cup superfine
    almond flour
1 tsp baking soda
1/2 tsp Himalayan salt
1 tbs cinnamon
1/4 tsp allspice
1/4 tsp ground cloves
1/2 cup coconut oil
1/2 cup Lakanto sweetener
4 eggs
1 tbs liquid espresso
    (fresh brewed)

Servings: 16

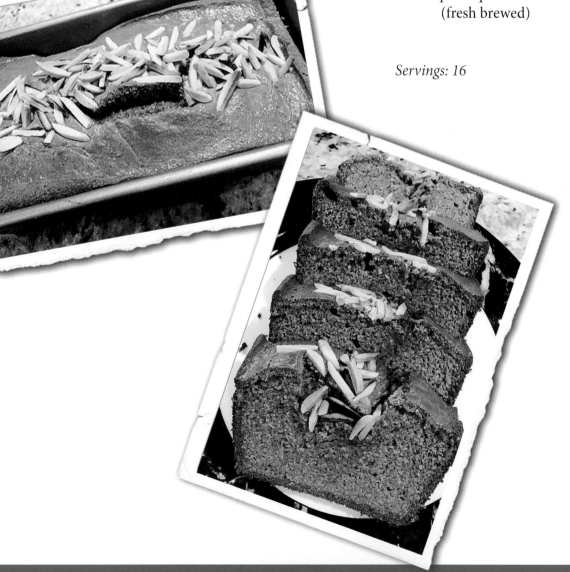

White & Dark Chocolate Covered Strawberries

Dark chocolate dip:

1. Using a double boiler melt chocolate chips on the top part and prepare the steaming hot water on the bottom. You can do the same thing if you don't have a double boiler, by placing a metal bowl on top of a pot

White chocolate dip:

1. Melt together cocoa butter and coconut oil over low heat in pot or in double boiler
2. Remove from heat and stir in vanilla flavored stevia drops

1. Dip strawberries in melted chocolate and place on a tray covered with wax paper
2. Place in refrigerator
3. Chill for at least 40 minutes
4. Serve chilled. This can be prepared a day in advance of a party or get together.

Ingredients:

24 Large strawberries

Dark chocolate dip:
8 Oz Lilly's Chocolate Chips

White chocolate dip:
1/4 Cup cocoa butter
1/4 Cup coconut oil
10 Drops vanilla Stevia liquid sweetener

Servings: 24

Pumpkin Nut Chocolate Chip Cake

1. Mix all ingredients in a cake mixer except for the nuts and chocolate chips until smooth
2. Stir in nuts and chocolate chips by hand and let sit for two minutes
3. Using a greased loaf pan fill in the pan with cake mix
4. Place in Preheated oven of 350
5. Put timer on 1 hour or until toothpick in center comes out clean

Ingredients:

2 Cups Almond Flour
1 Cup Coconut oil
1 Small 6 oz Can Unsweetened
        Pumpkin Puree
2 Cups Swerve Granular Sweetener
1 Tsp Cinnamon
2 Tsp Baking Soda
2 Tsp Baking Powder
2 1/2 Cups Lilly's Chocolate Chips
4 Eggs
4 Ounces toasted walnuts, chopped

Servings: 16

World's Best Chocolate Cake

This recipe is adapted from the original recipe created by Maida Heatter. Maida said this was her most famous recipe. It is known as the Queen Mother Cake because she made it for the Queen Mother who enjoyed it so much she requested it again. So I'm delighted to bring it to you. This is the world's best chocolate cake.

1. Preheat oven to 350
2. To make the cake: Butter a 9 or 10 inch springform pan and line the bottom with a round of wax paper or parchment paper. Butter the paper and dust with fine almond flour. Set aside.
3. Grind the nuts very finely in a food processor or use the equivalent amount of store-bought almond meal. I've made it both ways and it works.
4. In the top of a double boiler, over barely simmering water, melt the chocolate. Cover until partially melted and then uncover and stir until completely smooth. Remove from the heat to cool slightly.
5. In the large bowl of an electric mixer, cream the butter. Add the swerve or xylitol and beat for 2 minutes at medium-high speed. Add the egg yolks, one at a time, beating until well mixed after each addition. On low speed, add the chocolate and beat only to mix. Then add the almonds and beat only to mix, scraping down the sides of the bowl as needed.
6. If you have a second mixing bowl for your stand mixer or a hand held mixer as well, you can leave the batter in the bowl. Otherwise, transfer it to another large bowl and set aside. Wash your bowl and beaters and dry very well.
7. In a large bowl, (either the one you just washed or another one), add the salt to the egg whites and with clean beaters, beat the egg whites on high but only until they hold a definite shape, but are not stiff or dry. Stir a large spoonful of the beaten whites into the chocolate mixture to lighten it a bit and then fold in the rest of the whites in 3 additions.
8. Pour the mixture into the prepared pan and smooth the top, rotating the pan a bit to level the top. Bake for 20 minutes and then lower the oven 25° and bake for another 40-50 minutes. When cake is done, wet a kitchen towel, slightly wring it out, fold it and place it on the counter. Remove cake from the oven and place it directly on the towel. Let it stand for 20 minutes. Then remove the sides of the cake pan and place a wire rack over the top of the cake and invert it. Remove the bottom of the pan and the paper liner. Cover with another rack and invert the cake again and let it stand till completely cool on the wire rack.
9. If the center is sunken in, use a long, thin, sharp knife to make the top level, but be careful because the cake is a bit fragile. Prepare a cake plate, by placing 4 strips of wax paper around the outer edges of the plate, making a big square, to catch the frosting droppings and keep the cake plate neat looking. Set the cake upside down, centered, on top of the 4 strips.
10. To make the icing: In a medium heavy saucepan, scald the cream over medium heat until small bubbles form at the edges. Add the coffee and stir with a whisk to dissolve. Add the

chocolate and stir occasionally for about 1 minute. Remove from the heat and transfer the mixture to a bowl to stop it from cooking any further. Let the icing stand for about 15 minutes, stirring every now and then, until it's room temperature and has slightly thickened.

11. Stir the icing gently and pour it over the top of the cake. Use an offset spatula if you have one (a knife can work well too) to smooth the icing over the sides and around the cake. Smooth the top so that it looks evenly spread. Remove the 4 strips of paper carefully and after you've licked off the icing, discard. Serve cake as is or decorate with chocolate shavings Let cake stand for couple of hours so icing has time to solidify.

12. Cake keeps stored airtight at room temperature for 3-4 days.

Ingredients:

6 ounces almonds (1 1/4 cups), blanched or unblanched
6 ounces Lilly's Chocolate chips
1 1/2 sticks unsalted Kerrygold butter, at room temperature
3/4 cup swerve or xylitol
6 large eggs, separated
1/8 teaspoon salt

Icing:
1/2 cup heavy cream
1/2 teaspoon instant coffee
8 ounces Lilly's Chocolate chips

Servings: 12

Spice Cake

1. Preheat oven to 350 degrees
2. Cream together butter, swerve or xilitol, and Lakanto golden
3. Add coconut milk and almond flour
4. add eggs and vanilla extract, salt, baking soda, lemon rind and all spices
5. Pour into loaf pan. Bake for 40-50 minutes

Ingredients:

3 cups superfine almond flour
1 1/2 tsp. baking soda
1 tsp. Himalayan salt
1 1/2 tsp. cinnamon
3/4 tsp. nutmeg
1/4 tsp. powdered cloves
6 oz. softened unsalted
    Kerrygold butter
1 tsp. vanilla extract
1 1/4 cups Lakanto sweetener
1 cup sweetener
    (xylitol or swerve)
4 eggs
1 can full fat coconut milk
Finely grated rind of 1 lemon

Servings: 30

Moist Blueberry Cake

1. Preheat Oven to 375
2. Grease 9x12 inch pan at least 2inches deep with butter
3. In a cake mixer place butter, Lakanto, lemon extract and vanilla extract and mix for 2 minutes
4. Add eggs
5. In a separate bowl mix the almond flour, baking powder and salt
6. Using your cake mixer on low add the dry mixture until smooth
7. By hand add 1 1/2 cups of the blueberries
8. Gently pour the batter in the pan
9. Bake for 15 minutes
10. Remove and add the remaining 1/2 cup blueberries by sprinkling it over the top of cake
11. Put back in oven for 45 minutes until golden brown and a knife in the center comes out clean
12. Remove from oven and let cool one hour before serving

Ingredients:

1/2 Cup plus 3 Tbs unsalted butter room temperature
1 Cup Lakanto
1 Tsp lemon extract
1 Tsp vanilla extract
3 Extra large eggs whisked
1 2/3 cup almond flour
1 1/4 Tsp baking powder
1/8 Tsp salt
2 Cups blueberries

Servings: 16

Lemon Freeze

1. In a mixer using the egg whipping attachment, beat 1 cup Xylitol or Swerve with 4 egg yolks on low-medium until golden
2. Add the lemon juice and the lemon rind and beat again for a couple minutes on low
3. Pour mixture into a separate bowl and set aside
4. Wash out the bowl and whipping attachment and dry thoroughly
5. Using the mixer place 4 egg whites in the bowl and beat on high until it forms peaks
6. Very carefully pour egg & lemon sweetened mixture into the egg whites and fold by hand using a flexible spatula, gently until combined
7. Using either 12 mini ramekins or 1 large glass freezer safe container, pour mixture in and freeze overnight
8. Leave it out a minute or two and will scoop easily

Ingredients:

1 Cup Xylitol or Swerve
4 Eggs
1/2 Cup lemon juice
1/2 Tbs lemon rind

Servings: 12

Perfect Brownies

1. Preheat Convection Oven to 450 degrees
2. Butter a 9 1/2 by 9 1/2 pan
3. Mix Ingredients
4. Melt chocolate and butter over low heat in a double boiler
5. Stir in espresso
6. Set aside to cool
7. Mix eggs and salt and sweetener until very light and fluffy
8. Add the vanilla and almond extracts to the chocolate mixture
9. At a very slow speed fold the chocolate mixture into the egg mixture
10. Stir only with a spatula
11. Gradually add the almond flour until it's all mixed in
12. Add the optional nuts or Chocolate chips
13. Place in oven. Reduce oven temperature to 400 degrees
14. Bake for only 20-21 minutes. The top should be crispy brown.
15. Let cool. The insides should be gooey perfection

Ingredients:

6 oz of unsweetened
　　Lilly's Chocolate
2/3 of a cup grass fed butter
1 Tablespoon espresso
4 eggs
1/2 teaspoon of pink
　　Himalayan salt
2 cups Swerve or Xylitol
1 teaspoon Rodelle
　　vanilla extract
1/4 teaspoon Rodelle
　　almond extract
1 1/2 cup of extra fine
　　almond flour
1 1/2 cups of walnuts or pecans
　　(optional)
1/2 package Lilly's Chocolate
　　chips (optional)

Servings: 16

Hot Chocolate & Whipped Cream

1. In a pot heat up water and coconut milk and bring to a boil
2. Pour in blender
3. Add remaining ingredients except for the cinnamon and whipped cream
4. Blend well
5. Pour into your cup
6. Swirl whipped cream on top
7. Sprinkle cinnamon to your taste

Ingredients:

1/2 Cup filtered water
1/2 Cup unsweetened
    coconut milk
2 Tbs Unsalted Kerri Gold
    or organic butter
1 Tbs Bulletproof Brain Octane Oil
2 Tbs Unsweetened Ghirardelli
    Cocoa Powder
1/4 Tsp vanilla extract
A sprinkle of cinnamon
1/2 To 1 Dropper to taste of
    Stevia Sweet Drops
Whipped Cream to swirl on top
    (sugar free)

Servings: 1

Pecan Pie

1. Stir all ingredients together over low heat
2. Grease Pyrex baking cups with coconut oil
3. Pour in the mixture
4. Bake in a 350 degree oven for 35-40 minutes
5. Let cool and enjoy

Ingredients:

1 cup Lankanto Syrup
3 eggs
1 cup swerve sweetener
2 tablespoons of grassfed butter
1 teaspoon Rodelle No Sugar
      Vanilla Extract
1 1/2 cups of fresh pecans

Servings: 10 - 12

Helpful Hint:

I make this without a crust for simplicity and because Keto crusts leak. (A lot). You won't miss the crust.

Chocolate Caramel Cheesecake

1. Butter the Springform pan
2. Beat the eggs and xylitol together
3. Add cream cheese one tablespoon at a time until it's all creamy
4. Add the sour cream
5. Melt the Chocopefection Bars over a very low heat. Stir until melted
6. Blend into the cheesecake mixture
7. Melt the caramels over a very low flame. You might need to add a teaspoon of coconut oil to help it along
8. Drizzle the caramel on the top of the cheesecake. It will melt in
9. Bake your cheesecake at 375 degrees for just 30 minutes
10. Now, turn off your oven and leave your cheesecake in the oven for one hour
11. Remove and refrigerate
12. Cover each slice with a strawberry sliced or a single blackberry or raspberry

Ingredients:

3 8 oz packages of cream cheese (no sugar)
3 large eggs
2 cups full fat sour cream
1 cup of xylitol
3 Dark Chocolate Chocoperfection Bars
4 Tom and Jenny's Sugar Free Caramel Candy

Servings: 16

Chocolate Cupcakes with Chocolate Frosting

1. Preheat Oven to 350
2. Line Cupcake trays with individual paper cupcake cup liners
3. In mixer place coconut milk or almond milk
4. Add the Swerve sweetener, oil, and both extracts to mixture and beat in mixer until foamy
5. In a different bowl mix the almond flour, chocolate powder, baking soda and salt
6. Mix the two separate bowls together in the mixer until smooth
7. Pour into liners, filling 3/4 way
8. Bake 18-20 minutes until toothpick comes out clean
9. Allow to cool before putting frosting on top
10. Using mixer, cream together the butter and chocolate powder very well
11. Add the Swerve confectioners and mix well
12. Add in coconut milk and mix well
13. Add in vanilla
14. Mix until fluffy for 3 minutes
15. Use a frosting kit to swirl in a decorative manner

Ingredients:

1 Cup unsweetened almond
   or coconut milk
1 Cup Swerve Granular
1 Tsp Rodelle vanilla extract
1/2 Tsp Rodelle almond extract
1 1/2 Cups almond flour
1/3 Cup Bulletproof
   chocolate powder
3/4 Tsp baking soda
2 Tbs Coconut oil
1/4 Tsp salt
2 Eggs

Frosting:
1/2 Cup butter, softened
1/2 Cup Bulletproof
   chocolate powder
2 1/2 Cups Swerve Confectioners
3 Tbs coconut milk
1 1/2 Tsp Rodelle vanilla extract

Servings: 12

Peanut Butter & Chocolate Chip Turtles

This recipe was an accidental treasure find!
When you are in the mood for something a bit sweet, cold, creamy and gives you energy all at the same time and took one minute to put together and only needed 2 simple ingredients.

1. Use 1 teaspoon chocolate chips for every 1 tablespoon of peanut butter for each turtle
2. Combine both ingredients in a bowl for as many as you would like to make
3. Spoon mixture onto parchment paper lined trays, separated by an inch in between
4. If you want to make it more of a creamy chocolate turtle, melt some extra chocolate chips and pour over each turtle
5. If melting chocolate, pour over each turtle and immediately place tray in freezer
6. Remove tray after a minimum of 3 hrs

Ingredients:

Lilly's Chocolate Chips
All Natural No Sugar Added
Creamy Peanut Butter

Servings: varies

Pumpkin & Cinnamon Cake with Frosting

1. Preheat oven to 350
2. You may choose any cake mold you and your family enjoy for Halloween or Thanksgiving.
3. Whisk the coconut milk and vinegar in a small bowl and allow to sit and curdle
4. In a separate large bowl using a handheld cake mixer beat together the milk mixture, oil, Swerve and extracts. Add the flour, xantham gum, baking powder and soda, salt until smooth.
5. Depending on whether you are baking a large or small mold, bake for 20 minutes with small molds or until toothpick comes out clean in center and bake 30 minutes with a large mold or until knife comes out clean in center.
6. Frost when cool
7. Place Swerve confectioners, cinnamon, butter or oil, milk and vanilla in a bowl and use a handheld mixer . The color should be a honey brown color. If it looks too liquid then just add a little extra Swerve confectioners until desired consistency is reached.

Ingredients:

1 Cup unsweetened coconut milk
1 1/4 Cups Almond flour
1 Tsp apple cider vinegar
3/4 Tsp baking powder
1/2 Tsp baking soda
3/4 Tsp Xantham Gum
1/2 Tsp Pink Himalayan Salt
2 Tsp Vanilla Extract
1/4 Tsp Caramel extract
1 Tsp Cinnamon
1 Tbs Pumpkin pie spice
1/3 Cup coconut oil
3/4 Cup Swerve Granular

Cinnamon Frosting:
1/2 Cup Swerve Confectioners
1/2 Tsp cinnamon
2 Tbs butter or margarine melted
        or coconut oil
1 Tbs Unsweetened coconut milk
1/2 Tsp vanilla extract

Servings: 24

Chocolate "Happy Birthday" Cake

1. Preheat oven to 350
2. Using a cake mixer combine all of the dry ingredients
3. Add the remaining ingredients and mix until creamy
4. Grease two 9 inch round cake pans
5. Pour batter into the two cake pans
6. Bake between 20-35 minutes (please watch these cakes as every oven is so different from the other)
7. Remove from oven after a toothpick is tested in the middle and comes out clean
8. Allow to cool on cooling racks before frosting
9. Using mixer, cream together the butter and chocolate powder very well
10. Add the Swerve confectioners and mix well
11. Add in coconut milk and mix well
12. Add in vanilla
13. Mix until fluffy for 3 minutes
14. Spread frosting in between the two cakes and place one on top of the other
15. Frost the entire cake all around
16. With the remaining frosting, use a cake decorating set to design the top of your birthday cake with swirls and designs
17. Take a peeler and shave the 3 bars of chocolate into small shavings and place all over the sides of the cake
18. Place your candles on your cake and let the singing and cake eating party begin!

Ingredients:

Cake:
1 Cup Lakanto Syrup
1 Cup Coconut flour
1 Cup Bulletproof
    chocolate powder
1 Cup coconut oil
1 Tsp baking soda
16 Large eggs
1 Tsp Pink Himalayan Salt

Frosting:
1 Cup butter at room temperature
1 Cup Bulletproof
    chocolate powder
5 Cups Swerve Confectioners
6 Tbs Unsweetened coconut milk
3 Tsp Rodelle vanilla extract

Chocolate Shavings:
3 Lilly's Dark Chocolate Bars

Servings: 20

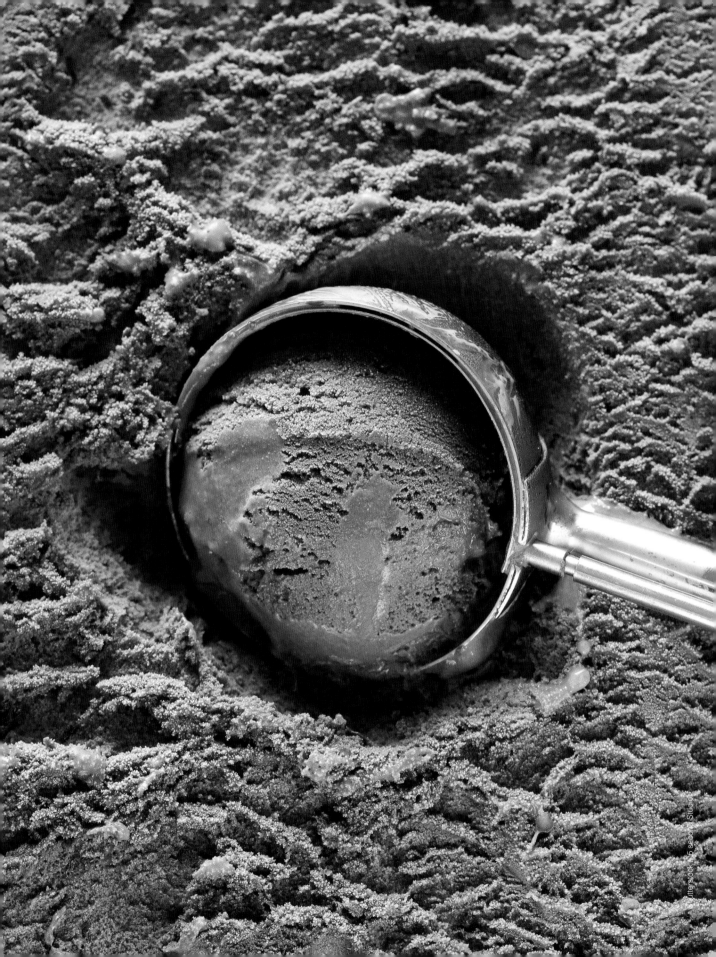

Incredibly Delicious Ice Cream

1. Gently mix all the ingredients
2. Add the mixture to your favorite ice cream maker
3. A serving is 1/2 cup - you should get 10 servings

Ingredients:

Perfect Vanilla Ice Cream:
2 1/2 cups heavy cream
8 egg yolks
1/2 cup xylitol (or swerve)
1 teaspoon vanilla extract

Perfect Chocolate Ice Cream:
2 1/2 cups heavy cream
8 egg yolks
1/2 cup xylitol (or swerve)
2 tablespoons of cocoa powder
dissolved in minimal hot water

Super Strawberry Ice Cream:
8 strawberries liquified in a blender or
VitaMix
2 1/2 cups heavy cream
8 egg yolks
3/4 cup xylitol (or swerve)

Espresso Coffee Ice Cream:
1 large cup of espresso
3 cups heavy cream
8 egg yolks
3/4 cup xylitol (or swerve)

Root Beer Ice Cream:
3 Cups heavy cream
2 Whole eggs
1 Egg yolk
3/4 Cup xylitol (or swerve)
1 Tsp vanilla extract
1 Tsp root beer extract

Pumpkin Ice Cream:
2 1/2 cups heavy cream
8 egg yolks
1/2 cup xylitol (or swerve)
3/4 cup unsweetened canned pumpkin
1 tsp ground nutmeg
1 tsp ground cinnamon

Shutterstock / 5 second Studio

Substitutions:

Non-Dairy Ice Cream:
Substitute 2 cans of coconut cream in place of the heavy
cream

Vegan Ice Cream:
Substitute 2 cans of coconut cream in place of the heavy
cream and omit the eggs

Chocolate Crinkle Cookies

1. Preheat oven to 350
2. Cover 2 Cookie sheets with parchment paper
3. Set aside
4. Using a mixer combine butter, swerve granular, almond flour, cocoa powder, eggs , vanilla, Xanthan gum and baking powder
5. Form 24 balls
6. Fill a plate with Swerve confectioner's sugar and toss each ball one at a time around the plate to coat very well
7. Lay on parchment paper
8. Leave room between the balls
9. Bake between 15-20 minutes depending on oven
10. Remove from oven
11. Cool on racks before putting away in containers to store

Ingredients:

1/2 Cup unsalted butter
2 Cups Swerve Granular
2 Cups Blanched Almond Flour
1 Cup Unsweetened Cocoa Powder
4 Large eggs
1 Tsp Vanilla Extract
2 Tsp baking powder
1/2 Tsp Xanthan Gum
Swerve Confectioner's Sugar

Yeilds: 24 cookies

Perfect Sorbet

1. Gently mix all ingredients together in a saucepan over a low flame
2. Cool
3. Add the mixture to your ice cream maker set to Sorbet mode
4. A serving is 1/2 cup

Ingredients:

Perfect Lemon Sorbet:
1 cup of water
1/2 cup xylitol (or swerve)
3/4 cup of lemon juice
Zest of half a lemon,
         finely chopped

Perfect Strawberry Sorbet:
1 cup of water
3/4 cup xylitol (or swerve)
2 pints of blended strawberries

Perfect Blueberry Sorbet:
1 cup of water
3/4 cup xylitol (or swerve)
2 pints of blueberries blended

Perfect Pineapple Jalapeño Tequila Sorbet:
1 cup of water
1 cup xylitol (or swerve)
1 oz of sugar free pineapple
         syrup
1 tablespoon of gold tequilla
Zest of 1 jalapeño,
         finely chopped

Servings: 10

European Grandmother's Almond Cookies

1. Preheat oven to 350
2. In a food processor combine almond flour, Swerve, egg, lemon zest and salt and pulse many times until becomes a sticky batter
3. Use a spoon to divide 24 equal size portions of cookie batter and then roll into individual balls
4. Spread cookie balls evenly onto greased baking sheet
5. Set aside
6. In a small heated skillet roast 24 almonds with a sprinkle of salt
7. Allow to cool
8. Place each almond in center of cookie ball by pushing down gently
9. Bake in oven between 13-15 minutes, depending on heat variations
10. Allow to cool completely
11. Using a sifter, lightly sprinkle some Swerve Confectioners Sweetener over the top of cookies
12. Store in airtight jar. Enjoy with a cup of tea or coffee

Ingredients:

2 Cups blanched almond flour
Zest from 1 whole lemon
2/3 Cup Swerve Granular
1/8 Tsp sea salt
1 Large egg
24 Almonds
Swerve Confectioners
    sweetener

Yields: 24 Cookies

Red Velvet Cupcakes and Cream Cheese Frosting

1. Preheat oven to 350
2. Prepare greased cupcake liners on the side in a cupcake mold tray. Set aside
3. Using a cake mixer bowl with electric whiskers, slowly whisk together all dry ingredients
4. Add all of the wet ingredients into the batter mix
5. Divide batter evenly into cupcake cup liners
6. Bake between 15-20 minutes depending on oven. Please watch them carefully as some ovens vary in temperatures
7. When a toothpick placed in the center comes out clean, it is ready
8. Remove from oven
9. Allow to cool
10. In a medium sized bowl, whisk together all frosting ingredients
11. Use a piping tip and bag to decorate cupcakes and sprinkle natural red powder over

Ingredients:

1/2 Cup Swerve Confectioner's Sweetener
1/2 Cup Coconut Flour
2 Tbs Bulletproof Unsweetened Chocolate Powder
1 Tbs Natural Red Food Dye
2 Tbs butter
4 Large eggs
1/4 Tsp Natural baking soda
1/4 Tsp Fine Pink Himalayan Salt

Cream Cheese Frosting:
1 Cup heavy cream
1 Tsp vanilla extract
10 Oz Cream cheese
1/2 Cup Swerve Confectioner's Sweetener
Dried Hibiscus Natural Flower Powder

Servings: 10 - 12

Grandma's Cheese Blintzes

Grandma Chaya was an amazing cook. She never followed a recipe. She did everything by feel and by taste.
There is NOTHING under the universe as good as these hot blintzes. **Warning: Seriously addictive.**
The crepes take some practice to make but once you've mastered the pouring of the crepe, you're set.

1. In a medium bowl mix the eggs, almond meal, vanilla extract, and cinnamon until combined. Make sure there are no lumps
2. Warm up a 9 inch frying pan on medium heat with butter. You don't want the butter to turn brown
3. Using a large spoon, pour the batter into the pan for one crepe. Lift the pan so the batter spreads around the pan. Try to keep it circular
4. Cook the crepe on one side well and then flip it over for 30 seconds on the other side. (My grandmother only cooked one side of the crepe)
5. Repeat until the batter is gone
6. Mix all the ingredients for the filling in a bowl with a spoon
7. Put a tablespoon of the mix in the middle of each crepe and fold it
8. Fold each side over the middle. Than fold down the tops
9. In a buttered pan over low heat cook until browned
10. Serve with sour cream and berries

Ingredients:

Crepe:
4 eggs
¼ cup almond meal
1 tsp vanilla extract
¼ tsp ground cinnamon
butter for frying

Filling:
1 lb farmer cheese
4 oz Philadelphia cream cheese
        not whipped, softened
1 egg
2 tblsp swerve

Yields: 8 - 10

Shutterstock / m.pilot

Index